# FUNNY YOU SHOULD SAY THAT

# FUNNY YOU SHOULD SAY THAT

## GERRY DEE

HarperCollinsPublishersLtd

Published by HarperCollins Publishers Ltd

First edition

HarperCollins books may be purchased for educational, business or sales promotional use through our Special Markets Department.

HarperCollins Publishers Ltd
Bay Adelaide Centre, East Tower
22 Adelaide Street West, 41st Floor
Toronto, Ontario, Canada
M5H 4E3

*www.harpercollins.ca*

Library and Archives Canada Cataloguing in Publication

Title: Funny you should say that / Gerry Dee.
Names: Dee, Gerry, 1968- author.
Identifiers: Canadiana (print) 20230481655 |
Canadiana (ebook) 2023048171X | ISBN 9781443465700 (hardcover) |
ISBN 9781443465717 (ebook)
Subjects: LCSH: Dee, Gerry, 1968- | LCSH: Comedians—Canada—Biography. |
LCSH: Comedians—Canada—Anecdotes. | LCSH: Stand-up comedy—
Canada—Anecdotes. | LCGFT: Autobiographies. | LCGFT: Anecdotes.
Classification: LCC PN2308.D38 A3 2023 | DDC 792.702/8092—dc23

Printed and bound in the United States of America

23 24 25 26 27 LBC 5 4 3 2 1

*To my biggest fans: Heather, Aly, Faith and Breton. Love you!*

# CONTENTS

# FUNNY YOU SHOULD SAY THAT

# PART ONE

**"Let's Be Honest, You're Not a Celebrity"**

# MY FIRST GIG

**M**ost comics will tell you that, for as long as they can remember, they were funny. They were the class clown, or always putting on funny skits at home, or always entertaining the grandparents when they visited for Sunday dinner. None of this was true with me. As a kid, I never even really knew what a stand-up comedian *was*. My family and I never watched them. We did, however, watch sitcoms. My parents would laugh hysterically at *The Honeymooners* and *All in the Family*. My sister loved *I Love Lucy* and *The Mary Tyler Moore Show*. I remember my brother losing it on the couch, watching *Hogan's Heroes*. The first shows *I* remember loving were *Family Ties*, *Three's Company*, *Cheers* and *SCTV*. So, I never really dreamt of being a comedian. A comedic actor, yes. I would've loved to do what Michael J. Fox or John Candy did for a living, though I kept that

3

ambition to myself, as my parents would have told me I was crazy.

My dad would often tell me: "Gerry, it is vain to think you're funny."

In fact, if I ever tried to be funny, it had *better* be funny, or my family would let me know. So I picked my spots carefully. My whole family was funny, so I had tough competition. I wouldn't say I was funny throughout any of my school years. I went to an all-boys school, and I carried on like any other boy at my school would do. I think we were all funny in our way. I would say I was more entertaining. *Amusing* might be a better word.

By university, I started to entertain more. To be honest, I think it was to make up for my appearance; when I reached university, girls entered the picture, and I sure wasn't going to win them over with my two massive front teeth and my 135-pound body. So I had to try with comedy. And sometimes, it worked.

When I was eighteen, I could do impersonations, mock others, tell a joke (more or less) and make faces. That was *it*. Still, it was enough that people started telling me, "You're so funny." And I liked hearing that. In fact, the more I heard it, the funnier I got. Yet I knew there was a big difference between that guy who could make others laugh at a party and that guy who could stand up on a stage, all by himself, and be funny *because he had to*. So, the idea of being a stand-up comic wasn't realistic for me. And yet, the idea didn't go away.

One day in 1992, I pulled into a Canadian Tire on my way to Yarmouth, Nova Scotia—I was living in Halifax and working for Molson at the time—and bought a hand-held tape recorder. I'd talk into it while driving, and in this way I started to flesh out some ideas for bits. They were all basic premises, and fairly shopworn. Still, I thought they were funny, and I began to dream about trying stand-up. I didn't have the nerve. I took the tape I'd made while driving around and put it in a box, where it stayed, on my desk, for seven years.

I went to York University for five years—I needed an extra year to get my degree—and teachers' college for another two years at St. Francis Xavier University. In 1994, I became a substitute teacher. From 1995 to 2003, I taught history, and then physical education, at De La Salle College, a Catholic high school in Toronto. Yet the notion of becoming a comic refused to go away: I was moonlighting at The Keg, and there was another waiter who worked there who was an actual working comic named Michael. He and I used to do bits for each other. Whenever "Beat It" came on the in-house sound system, I'd do my Michael Jackson impression. Quite often, I'd ask Michael about his life as a comic. Whenever I did, he'd always ask me the same thing: "Man, why don't you try it?"

I was also funny in the classroom as a teacher. It was a way, I discovered, to make your students pay attention. I remember one Grade 12 kinesiology class where I was riffing about something. That's when it happened—the moment that set off my whole career. A student named Peter yelled out, "Sir, have you ever thought of trying stand-up comedy?"

There it was, the nudge I needed.

"I tell you what," I told him. "I promise to try it by the end of the year."

Now, it wasn't as though they were all invested in making sure that I followed up on this promise. But *I* was. It was more a promise to myself.

At the time, everything I knew about the world of stand-up comedy came from Michael at The Keg, who told me that Yuk Yuk's held an open mic every Monday night. In order to get on, you had to phone the club before 3 p.m. and get your name on a list. Then you phoned back around four o'clock to see if you'd been picked to perform that night. Yet Michael warned me that no one gets picked the very first time they call.

"You just have to keep doing it," he told me. "You have to phone week after week after week. After you do it about eight times, you may get picked. It's just what you have to do."

So, I called and left my name. I had begun the process. Now I had about eight weeks to get my first five minutes ready. I felt very powerful. I had thought about this for years and had finally made that first step. Since I didn't want anyone to know I was doing this, especially anyone at my school, I didn't want to use my real name. This meant I had to come up with a stage name on the spot— and the moniker that flew into my head was the one I still use to this day: Gerry Dee. (My real name is Gerard Donoghue.) I was sure to spell the name—D-E-E—since using the single letter, *D*, struck me as something that only a big star would do, like the singer Stevie B.

I didn't even bother to phone back at 4 p.m. to see if I got on, for two reasons. The first was that Michael told me it would take about eight weeks. The second was that I didn't want to go on. *This*, if nothing else, should indicate my level of commitment. And yet, just after four, I got a call from Michael (who had called in to see if *he* got up) and he was like, "Oh man! You got on! They picked you, man!"

"But you told me it'd take eight weeks . . ."

"I know, I know, it's a complete fluke. Maybe they were a bit short this week, sometimes it happens, but either way, you're going on tonight."

I had to be there at eight. That meant I had four hours to cobble together a five-minute set from a bunch of half-finished jokes I'd written on various pieces of paper, little comic premises I promised myself I'd flesh out one day. So there I was, trying to put them into some semblance of order, just to give myself something that even came close to being an "act." When I was done, I told exactly two people that I'd be appearing: a pair of brothers named James and John who were friends of mine.

So, I went to the club. I walked in the door. I saw that, instead of writing down "Gerry Dee" on the performers list, *as I had spelled it*, they'd written "Gerry D." Immediately, I started worrying that the other comics would all think I was too big for my britches. It was a ridiculous concern, since they all had far, far bigger things to worry about. Then again, I was freaking out. I had never been so nervous. Mark Breslin, the head of Yuk Yuk's, was there. Maybe that had something to do with it? I can't say. I was completely taken by surprise by my panic. I had never been a nervous public speaker. I did it all day and every day in front of my students. And yet, a part of me realized that if I was this nervous, it had to be because this venture—this standing up in front of other people and trying to make them laugh—meant something to me.

The MC was a comic named Jack who had been on the scene for years. I remember thinking that Jack was the guy I had to impress, as *he* was the man who would advance my career. I would later find out that Jack was just another comic who picked up the gig to make an extra fifty bucks that night.

I was the ninth of sixteen comics. Just before I went on, Jack started making fun of my name—"Gerry D? Really? Gerry D? What the *fuck* kind of name is that?" He wasn't wrong; it looked so stupid. It was my first time onstage and my name on the sheet looked like I was already a star. Hearing this, I made a decision. I wasn't going to do this. I was going to walk out and never show my face in Yuk Yuk's or any other comedy club again in my entire life. One second after making that decision, I made another: if I didn't go on, I'd never forgive myself. So, yes, I would go on. I might spectacularly bomb, but at least I'd have done it. I'd have fulfilled my promise to myself and my students and, at the same time, gotten the comedy bug out of my system.

So I went on, trembling.

My first joke started, "So, my brother is twenty-six and still leaves me voice messages like this . . ." I imitated the messages. Crickets. The next bit was no funnier. There were more crickets. None of it was funny. At least I had a big finish: I'd arranged with some technician to play the song "Say You, Say Me" by Lionel Ritchie, to which I'd lip-synch and do a stupid dance. Yet when it came time for the song to play, there was nothing. I looked helplessly toward the control room. That's when I heard a voice come over the club's intercom: "Sorry, man. Breslin's in the office, talking to someone, so we can't turn your tape on. You're done."

And done I was. Done like dinner. It was the greatest defeat I'd ever had. I stared at the audience. They stared back at me. I put down the microphone and slumped off, my humiliation complete. If there was a consolation, it was knowing that I would never, ever have to do this again. That's when something interesting happened. Just as I was stepping off the stage, another one of the comics at the back yelled out, "Stick to teaching!"

I paused. I remember thinking, *Who are you to tell me to stick to teaching?* Right there and then, I swore to myself that I *would* do this again, and that I'd either get better at stand-up or die trying. This promise to myself was only strengthened a few minutes later, when another comic tried to make me feel better by saying, "You know, you really weren't too bad for your first time. Of course, you *do* know that you have to do it for at least five years before you make a nickel, don't you?" My reaction was the same: if you think I'm going to go five years without making money from comedy, you are out of your mind.

Looking back, I have to say it was a strange sequence of events. One minute after having performed what might very well be the biggest bomb in the history of comedy, I was now determined not only to continue doing it, but to make money doing it. So I kept at it. I played every Monday night for which I was picked. I got better. In 2001, I entered a competition called Toronto's Funniest Person with a Day Job. My set was full of silly, hacky stuff, all my teacher bits with a few rubbery faces thrown in for good measure. I came first anyway, winning five hundred dollars and, more importantly, a spot at Just for Laughs in Montreal (more about that in chapter 3). It was one of the first, and only, times my dad saw me perform live. After I won, he jokingly said, "I had you fifth."

I *think* he was joking.

# IN CARS

**W**hen it comes to cars, I'm not the sort of guy who cares about the latest makes and models, who knows anything about engine specifications, or who cares one whit about performance statistics—acceleration, braking time, top speed. It's all white noise, at best. If I classify as a car guy, it's because I've always had one. I feel naked without one.

When I was eighteen, my dad gave me his 1979 Plymouth Volaré so that I could get to and from York University. (He didn't actually *give* it to me; he let me use it, which was better, since he still paid the insurance. Meanwhile, he had to take a bus to work, at which point he would then drive a bus, often the same one he'd just taken. It was one of those things that only a parent would do.) I remember it well because it was also the first car I had to go on dates with girls. If I was ever trying to win them over with a fancy car, this was not it. Burgundy just read as boring, so any time I pulled up for a date, I wasn't off to the best start. The brown rust spots didn't help, either. I'm not even sure they make cars in burgundy anymore, and I can see why. But at least I knew that if a girl liked me, it was for me and not my car.

After that, I got a blue 1982 Ford Mustang, for which I paid five hundred dollars. I was getting a little closer to the normal colour spectrum for cars, but it was *baby* blue, so it didn't exactly reek of cool. Then, I got a green Pontiac Sunfire, although this one was a convertible. Why a Sunfire? They were terrible cars, so I could get one for cheap. Why green? Nobody else would buy it, so I got a bit of a deal. Why a convertible? Because I thought it made up for the brand and colour of the car. It didn't. My reputation for masculinity took a major hit with my friends. And as with the Volaré, if I ever got a date, I knew she liked me for me, because the car certainly oozed "I have no money."

Later, as I earned more, I would get a better car each time my lease ran out. And after I was married and we added kids to the mix, fun cars gave way to practical cars. That's when the minivan enters the picture, the true marker of a married person with kids. So, yes, my car was new now, but it screamed, "I have a wife and kids." I skipped the whole "cool car" phase of life that some people get to have.

But at the end of the day, they were just machines to get me from point A to point B, and most of those points would be comedy gigs as my career was developing. They were just cars, and I always had to have one.

My point is: no single thing has benefited my career more than car ownership. It is extremely hard to make any money in comedy, which means that a lot of comics are flat broke. They don't even own a car, or have any way to make it to their gigs. Some comics I know don't even have a driver's licence. And yet, when I was starting out, I always had a job—be it waitering or teaching or coaching hockey—that earned me enough money to have some sort of car. I was lucky. I could drive. I could give other comics a lift. Agents and club owners were constantly putting me on bills I had no right being on, for the simple reason that I could give the other comics—many of them funnier and more established than myself—a lift to the gig. I was Uber for comics before Uber existed.

I've driven all over the country. I've driven in snow, rain, sleet and sunshine. I've driven all night to get home for my teaching job in the morning. I can't tell you how many times I made it home at dawn, grabbed an hour's nap, cleaned myself up and spent the whole day teaching.

It's those in-between cities that are the worst. If you've got a gig in Thunder Bay, that's fourteen hours of driving, so you'd take a plane, the cost of which would likely be more than you'd be paid for the gig. Then there's that gig at the back of a restaurant in Pickering. Pickering is an hour, more or less, from my house. Obviously, you drive. The problem is the Windsors of the world. Or the Ottawas or Cornwalls or Sudburys. I'm talking about the cities that are five or six hours away. With them, you have a conundrum: Do you do the gig, leave at midnight and drive through the night? Or do you eat up any profit by grabbing a hotel? In the mind of that working, low-level comic, where money is always the first consideration, you drive. You just do. If there's one consolation, at least you'll have company.

The year was 2000, and it was my first-ever paid Yuk Yuk's gig. I had just signed with them, and this was a proud moment for me. I got a call from head office with the details and was asked if I could drive the headliner. I didn't know him, but then again, I knew virtually none of the comics. "Sure, I'll drive him."

I was so excited about this gig. I was about eighteen months into my stand-up career and now that I'd signed on with Yuk Yuk's, I was officially becoming a road comic. More bookings like this would start to come in. Some would be in clubs, and some would be what we call "one-nighters," like this one, where you drive in and drive out the same day. They could be a hockey fundraiser, a company party or any event, really, where the organizers had hired one to three comics to perform. This one was just me and the headliner. What a great opportunity to meet another comic who was way more established than me and made a living doing this. Keep in mind, I was still teaching, so comedy was my side hustle, as they call it. It would be great to pick his brain, maybe ask some questions or get some advice.

On the night of the gig, I picked up this headliner at Yonge Street and Lawrence Avenue, which was around the corner from the condo where I lived in North Toronto. He nodded and got in. He didn't say anything. I learned nothing about him—he just sat there, staring out the window,

14

chewing gum. For the first hour, I tried asking him questions. Had he done this event before? Does it get a good crowd? In return, I got sullen, one-word answers: yup, sometimes, nope. He reminded me of the blond kidnapper in *Fargo*, though instead of smoking, he kept putting fresh pieces of gum in his mouth. After an hour, I just gave up, and we drove the rest of the way in silence.

After the gig, we got back in the car and I drove the two hours back to Toronto in complete silence. At Yonge and Lawrence, he got out. He didn't thank me or offer to chip in for gas. I never forgot that. Ever. I have no idea why he treated me this way, but my only assumption is that he felt I was competition to him. Another comic added to the roster who hadn't, in his mind, paid his dues. Who knows? But it became a theme as I worked more and more. Drive around comics who were often miserable. I used to show up at De La Salle and my buddies on staff would joke about my gig the night before. "You know you get gigs because you drive, right?" they would tease. They weren't wrong. Who knew that having a car would play such a big role in how much work I would get as a comic?

There were these two comics whom I was constantly being asked to drive. They knew everything about comedy. They liked nobody, and nobody was funny but them. These were long drives. The guys were the epitome of comics on the grind—they were never going to get any better, they were never going to get any worse, and on some level, they knew it. As for why I always seemed to get stuck driving them, I later learned that they'd already worked their way through every other comic who happened to own a car. They were the polar opposite of the first guy I drove to London—they talked incessantly, and everything that came out of their mouth was a complaint. The car was too noisy. The seats weren't comfortable. They wanted to stop for coffee. They wanted to keep going. It was too hot in the car. Then it was too cold. The club we were going to was shit. The club owner was shit. Their agents were shit and the comedy scene in Canada was shit, shit, shit. When they weren't bitching about every little thing that crossed their minds, they were telling me how shitty *my* act was—how this story wasn't funny, how I needed to do more of that, how I should pay attention to their acts if I wanted to see how a real pro got things done. I paid attention. I learned nothing.

One night, I was invited to play a gig at this company event in Mississauga. As usual, I only got the gig because I was one of the few comics still willing to be a chauffeur. Still, it was an attractive offer: I'd get fifteen minutes as the opener, at a time when I rarely got a chance to do more than five. So even though I dreaded the idea of being trapped in a car with this comic, I agreed, as it was only a thirty-minute drive.

The gig was at seven. I arranged to pick him up at my usual spot, the northwest corner of Yonge and Lawrence, at six, thinking that an hour would be plenty of time to get us out there. I showed up on time. He wasn't there. I waited. Five minutes went by. I started calling him. No answer. Ten minutes went by. I phoned again. Still no answer. At 6:15, I resorted to phoning a comic named Ian Sirota, who worked at Yuk Yuk's. He was the only comedian I knew, as we had worked at The Keg together.

"Ian. There's a problem. The comic I'm supposed to drive is not here."

"What do you mean?"

"I was supposed to pick him up at six. He still hasn't shown up."

"Call him."

"I did. He's not answering."

"Gerry, you gotta leave. There's nothing else you can do."

"So, who's gonna do his half-hour?"

"You'll have to."

"But what about my fifteen?"

"You'll do both."

"*What?*"

"You'll do the full forty-five."

"But I don't *have* forty-five minutes."

"Well, you're just going to have to do it."

I left. I faked my way through forty-five minutes. There was a lot of ad-libbing and interaction with the audience—"You, sir . . . yes, you. Where are you from? What do you do for a living? Is that your wife, by any chance?"

By the time I got home, there were fourteen messages on my answering machine. From the headliner. They started out somewhat cordial. "Hi, Gerry, it's 7:05, just wondering where you are?" Then he started to get testy: "Gerry. It's a quarter after seven. Where in the hell are you?" Finally, he got irate: "Goddamn it, Gerry, you were supposed to drive me. I've never seen such unprofessional behaviour. I'm gonna talk to Yuk Yuk's about this. You owe me three hundred dollars for the money I was supposed to make. This is unacceptable." By the last phone call, he was attempting to backtrack. "Ha ha, looks like we *both* made a mistake, didn't we, Gerry? Looks like the start time was seven and not eight, ha ha. I bet they were wondering what happened to us." I wasn't laughing.

I called him up that night. He was still awake. I told him the gig had been at seven, that we'd arranged to meet at six, that he was the one who'd messed it up, and that, far from missing the gig, I'd done his thirty minutes for him. "Oh, and one other thing: I'm done. I'll never, *ever* drive you to a gig again."

And I never did. It was at that moment that I called my agent at Yuk Yuk's and literally gave him a list of names I would never drive again. "If it means I don't get the gig, that's fine, but I can't do this anymore."

On top of all that, the driving is dangerous. The graveyards of the world are filled with comics and musicians who left a gig in the middle of the night, and it was snowing, and the last thing they should've been doing was driving non-stop to make it home for their day job in Toronto. Around 2004, I was booked to play at a peach festival in Winona, Ontario. Also playing was a comic named Angelo Tsarouchas. Angelo, unlike these other comics I have mentioned, was a good guy, and we decided to drive up together. We weren't looking forward to the gig. It was one of those day-long events in the middle of nowhere, when you'd be competing with pony rides, puppet shows, midway barkers and mosquitoes. Meanwhile, couples with baby strollers would pass by your tent, stop, listen for thirty seconds and move on. But the peaches were phenomenal.

At a certain point, I had to turn onto a rural road. It went on forever: no bends, no intersections, no markers of any kind. Angelo and I got to talking. Finally, after forty-five minutes on this road, there was a stop sign. The cross street, meanwhile, was a two-lane highway on which the cars were travelling at sixty miles an hour. By that point, I must have been lulled into a trance. Angelo, I remember, was telling a story, and I was laughing, and it felt like that stop sign—which would have been in my line of vision for the past fifteen minutes—seemed to pop into view at the very last moment. I braked too late. Knowing I wasn't going to stop in time, I hit the gas, thinking I could make it through a hole in the traffic. I couldn't—out of the left side of my field of vision, I spotted an SUV barrelling toward me.

It's funny how time really does slow down in these situations. I remember thinking, *That SUV is going to hit us*. Then I thought, *That SUV is going to kill me*. In that split second, I took in my surroundings: there were clouds, fields, cows. I cranked the wheel to the right, hoping at the very least to take the impact on the rear of the car. The other driver swerved as well. We missed each other by inches. I rolled to a stop. Neither Angelo nor I could speak. Weirdly, we were only about three minutes away from the peach festival. We drove the rest of the way in absolute silence.

Ten minutes after arriving, I was onstage, batting away flies, ignoring the smell of grilled meat and trying to be funny. It's hard to be funny anytime, let alone when you have the sun blinding you and the sound of cows mooing in the background. Or were they laughing? Who knows? I was still sweating from the terror of almost dying a few minutes earlier, so the sweat from the sun just seemed to blend in.

Today, I no longer drive comics to gigs. It's not that I absolutely, categorically refuse to drive other comics. It's just that I don't need to anymore. I fly to a lot of gigs now. I'm often the headliner, with the support comic coming from someplace else. On the rare occasion that I do drive to a gig, and there's an opening comic coming from Toronto as well, I'll tell them that I'll see them there. It's nothing personal. I have things to do. I tape every gig, and when I'm driving to a show, I like to listen to the tape of the previous night's performance. It helps me gauge what's working and what still needs to be punched up. Or I'll get some thinking done. Or I'll make phone calls.

The bottom line is that those first few years were a grind. Everyone had to take their turn driving the comics who were mean or a pain in the ass. Once you got better than them, you passed this torch on to the next young comic. Eventually, these comics were on everyone's "don't drive them" list. So, if you plan on being a comic and you plan on being an asshole, you'd better get your own car or get ready to take the bus or the train quite often.

# MY FIRST
# JUST FOR LAUGHS

After I'd been doing stand-up for about a year, I set my sights on a competition called Toronto's Funniest Person with a Day Job. The attraction here was that the winner got a spot at Just for Laughs in Montreal, the biggest and most prestigious comedy festival in the world. It was all part of an absurd fantasy I had at the time. I'd win Toronto's Funniest Person, then I'd kill in Montreal. *Then*, I'd get a development deal for my own sitcom. If it could happen to Ray Romano and Tim Allen—both of whom got a TV show after a landmark set at Just for Laughs—I figured it could happen to me. This, believe it or not, is the way I saw things.

Toronto's Funniest Person was held at the old Laugh Resort, which at the time was operating out of a Holiday Inn on King Street. There were about thirty other contestants, most of whom did the sort of clichéd bits that co-workers find funny, if only because it relieves the tedium. There were contestants who performed zany dances; *my* moves were culled from shifts at the famed Crocodile Rock bar in Toronto, where I danced on the bar every time the song "Beat It" by Michael Jackson came on. There were contestants who went with broad impersonations; mine was of my Scottish father. There were contestants who went big with physical shtick. Again, I was no different. At the time, I was doing a horrible bit about how hard it is to meet women when you're drinking through a straw. This involved a lot of tongue contortions, and not much else.

I wasn't very funny, and if I won that day, it was because the other people in the contest were even *less* funny. I never stopped to consider that. I suppose I was distracted because my appearance on Just for Laughs was coming up.

September rolled around. I drove to Montreal with an old friend of mine named John Macciocchi who also taught high school. John and his brother James were so supportive of me. They came to so many shows in my early years. As well, I could bounce ideas off John, as he was also very funny. After five or six hours in the car, we got to the Montreal Hilton, the hotel that always acts as sort of ground zero for the festival. All of the comics stayed there, all of the agents stayed there, and all of the Just for Laughs press conferences were held there. I'd been given a double room of my own, which went a long way toward convincing me that I belonged there.

John and I checked in and went to our room. It was nice. There was a mini-bar and a hair dryer. I decided to leave

John there and go find the Just for Laughs office, where I would sign in. Again, I can't stress enough how excited I was. I remember how badly I wanted to put on a Just for Laughs lanyard, which would identify me as one of the performers. I couldn't wait to reach into a Just for Laughs swag bag, if only to see what a Just for Laughs performer might get. I was dying to open the program and see my name on the same page as some of the biggest comics on earth. Most of all, I couldn't wait to find out when I'd be performing on that huge stage, in that huge auditorium, in front of those glaring white lights that spelled out Just for Laughs.

The office, it turned out, was in a suite on the main floor. There were a lot of people in the room, and they were all talking to one another. There was a table at one end, with fruit and coffee and bottles of San Pellegrino. I approached the woman at the check-in table.

"*Bonjour*," she said.

"Hi," I told her. "I'm appearing at the festival."

"Great!" she said. "And what's your name?"

"Gerry Dee. That's D-E-E."

She started looking. At first, I wasn't worried, since hundreds of comics appear at the festival, and if she couldn't find my name immediately, it must have been because the names weren't sorted alphabetically. She looked through her list. She looked through her list again. She looked up at me, concerned. "Hmm, I don't seem to be able to find it. You said it was spelled D-E-E?"

"Yes, that's it."

She looked again. "Hmm," she said. "Give me a second."

She got up and started speaking in French to another woman. That woman came over and introduced herself. "I understand you're appearing with us?" she stated, though in a way that made it sound like a question.

"Yes," I told her. "I won Toronto's Funniest Person with a Day Job."

"I see." Pause. "And what is that?"

"It's a contest," I mumbled. "At the Laugh Resort?"

"I tell you what," she said. "Why don't you return to your room, and I'll look into it. Then I'll give you a call when I hear something?"

"Okay," I said.

I went back upstairs. John was there. I told him what happened.

"It must be some kind of mistake."

"I know," I said.

By now, I was worried and confused. I was worried that I had come here for nothing, and I couldn't figure out how they didn't know I was there. Were they not aware of the contest? I had my room; how did they not have my lanyard? It was all about the lanyard. I guess it was some kind of validation for me. Like my comedy trophy, in some ways. With all of this weighing on me, I decided to go back down to the lobby and see if maybe they'd found it; patience is the enemy of someone with ADHD. I went back down the elevator, passed lots of comics wearing their lanyards, and went into the same registration room. There, I asked the same people the same questions and headed back upstairs to my room with the same answers. They had nothing stating that

I was in the festival. Then things got worse. I arrived back at my room, where John was waiting.

"Guess who called?" he asked.

"Who?"

"Brent Schiess. He sounded important. And pissed off."

Brent was the manager of programming for the entire festival.

"What?!" I said.

"Yeah. He called. Right after you left."

"Jesus, John, what did he say?"

"Not much." He grinned. "I told him I was your manager."

"You . . . sorry?"

"I told him I was your manager, and that there was a problem."

"John. Why would you do that? Comics don't have managers after six months!"

"I dunno," he said, still grinning. "I thought it would make you sound bigger."

The phone rang. This time, it was Ellen, the owner of the Laugh Factory. Usually, I'd be pleased to hear from her. Not this time.

"Gerry," she said, "what is going on there? I got a call from Brent. He said you were bothering everyone, looking for your festival package?"

"Well, 'bothering' is a strong word. I was just trying to check in and get my lanyard and stuff."

"Please call Brent and straighten this out."

So I called.

"Look," he said. "You need to understand something.

You're not a part of Just for Laughs. Your name's not in the program, you don't get a free pass for all of the events and you don't get a lanyard."

"Oh."

"We're giving you a spot at one of the side venues. You'll get five minutes."

Ouch. That call hurt. I had been put in my place.

"Okay," I said. "Five minutes."

That night, I went to a club called ComedyWorks. It held about eighty people; the vast majority were there to see the other eight comics who'd be appearing. To see me, there were exactly two people. The first was John. The second was Michael, who I had worked with at The Keg. I should also add that, by this point, my dream of being a sitcom star had pretty much vanished. In all the excitement, I had forgotten an important fact: Ray Romano and Tim Allen had been gala acts, performing on the biggest night, and on the biggest stage, of the festival. On the other hand, here I was, about to do five minutes at a small, out-of-the-way club. As I looked at the rest of the lineup, it occurred to me that, even here, I was punching above my weight: all the other comics were seasoned professionals, many of them well known. Furthermore, they were using ComedyWorks as a warm-up, and they would appear a half-dozen other times at the festival. Not me—my five minutes that night would be my only performance.

I went on fifth. The MC's introduction was: "This guy won a little contest in Toronto, so we're going to let him come up and do five minutes."

I did my Scottish Dad impersonation, I did my "picking up girls with a straw in your mouth" bit, I did my funny dancing. I received polite applause. It would've been better if I'd bombed; at least then I would've stood out. The comic who went on after me was a guy named Dave Attell, who is extremely well known today: he's appeared on most of the late-night shows and had a recurring guest spot on Pete Holmes's series *Crashing*. He destroyed that night. Not only did he destroy, but he did it with a bit about a guy walking down the street, holding a bunch of balloons. That was it—I couldn't believe he could be so funny with a story about some guy holding on to balloons. Yet it was silly and absurd and very, very funny. And his delivery was impeccable. The audience loved him. I sat at the back and watched. It was depressing. I thought I was funny until I saw Dave Attell.

That's when I had an epiphany. For the first time since I'd started doing stand-up, I realized that I wasn't that funny. I might have been funny-guy-at-work funny. But I was light years away from being professional-comic funny. And things got worse. With the night drawing to a close, Michael went up to the manager and said, "Hey, I'm a comic from Toronto. You mind if I go on?"

The guy looked at Michael and said, "Sure, why not?"

In getting a spot, just like that, Michael completely invalidated my triumph at Toronto's Funniest Person with a Day Job. He went on and killed. His impressions were amazing. Afterward, he asked the owner, Jim, if he could go on during the late show as well. Jim said yes. I stepped

27

up and asked the same thing and he said they were full. My night was over. I would stay and watch Michael kill. Again.

I went back to Toronto, thankful I still had a day job. At this point, I was pretty much thinking that I'd pack it in; I never, ever wanted to feel like I'd felt in Montreal again. But then, a couple of nights later, I flipped on the TV, and there was Dave Attell on *Letterman*, fresh from his appearance at Just for Laughs. He was doing his balloon-guy bit. For some reason, the bit just wasn't working on national television. At first, I couldn't figure out why. But then it came to me: on TV, Attell couldn't swear. Without the swearing, the bit had lost its edge. This I found weirdly encouraging. He still did well, but it wasn't as good as when I saw him live. I guess you could say I had some hope again.

I decided to give comedy another year. Back then, I was always telling myself this. Another year, and then I'll see. Another year, and I'll reassess. Eventually, the day came when I wasn't telling myself that anymore.

I lost touch with Michael. He moved out west. What I do know is that I never would have tried stand-up comedy without his guidance, support and encouragement. I'm still close with John and James Macciocchi. The same can be said about those two brothers; their support and friendship all these years helped me get through many tough gigs and moments of doubt, most of all just by showing up.

I also learned to never do a bit about balloons. Dave Attell had that one covered quite well.

# CITY OF ANGELS

In 2002, I won the San Francisco International Comedy Festival, an international event in which most, if not all, of the other competitors were full-time comedians. Yet I was still a teacher, and I can clearly remember the other comics laughing when they discovered this. One of them was a stand-up named Sam Tripoli. (Today, he's best known as the host of a half-dozen podcasts, most notably *Tin Foil Hat*, *Broken Simulation* and *Cash Daddies*—really, he's the hardest-working man in the world of podcasting.)

"Dude," he told me, "you can't be up in Canada, wasting your days teaching. You gotta be here, in Los Angeles. It's silly that you have a job, still. So, for Christ's sake, quit your job and get your ass down here."

This made an impression. At the time, I had an agent I used for Canadian gigs. His name was Evan Adelman, and I always used to ask him, "When should I quit my day job?"

"You'll know," he told me.

"I'll know?"

"Yes. You'll just know. Plus, you'll be able to afford it."

I thought about this as well. Between teaching, corporate stand-up gigs and my hockey school (more on that later), I made about $120,000 a year. This felt like a lot of money, especially since I had no real financial obligations apart from payments on my one-bedroom condo. I also had $40,000 in the bank. As far as I was concerned, I had more than enough money to fund myself while I broke into the business down in California.

Then I considered my teaching career. I'd been at it for nine years. I had a new passion, now. Though comedy never affected my work—or, at least, I don't *think* it affected my work—it was true that, at times, I really had to juggle. I was always asking for a day or two off when I had to travel, and I was always having to ask other teachers to cover for me.

I went to the school principal, a Christian Brother named Domenic Viggiani.

"Brother," I said, "I want to take a year off."

"Okay," he said.

"I'm going to go to Los Angeles for a year. Everyone tells me the same thing—that if you're going to make it in comedy, you have to do it full-time, and LA is the place to make it big."

He completely understood. He was so good to me as I pursued this dream, and though it had rarely affected my teaching commitments, I could see it was starting to. I also knew that if it didn't work out, he would find a way to hire me back.

That was in May. I had my goodbye party at a bar called Up in downtown Toronto. I invited everyone I knew—friends, family, teachers, other comics. It was a going-away party for an up-and-coming comedian who was about to leave his family, friends and financial security at the age of thirty-four to chase a dream. With that in mind, maybe a place called Up wasn't the best location for it.

Was I saying goodbye forever? It could very well be. I wasn't planning to go to LA and fail, so forever was my intention. It went to the early hours. I remember making a bit of a speech, in which I told everybody how much they meant to me.

A few days later, I found myself in the departure lounge at Toronto's Pearson International Airport, crying. I'd already found the three things that my mum had snuck into my luggage: a prayer book, a Miraculous Medal that I still wear to this day, and a heartfelt note telling me how much she would miss me. My folks were getting on, and it could very well be that I'd only see them once or twice a year from this point on. It hit me hard. And so I mailed them a letter to make sure they knew what they meant to me. Saying it face to face wasn't something we did in our Scottish household. We all knew how much we loved each other, but we never said it.

I know my parents were concerned that I was leaving teaching to make this move. I have a feeling they didn't find me that funny, but I also know they didn't want to hold me back. And in some ways, I really feel I'm not that funny, but that's a good thing, as it always makes me want to work harder.

Still sniffling, I got on a plane and went to Los Angeles. One week after I arrived, my mother sent me a card with these words: "I'm so happy that you are following your dreams." At that point, I knew I had their blessing.

My friend Mike Wardlow told me that there was an apartment available in his building. I took it, even though it was a two-bedroom. I figured the empty room would come in handy for visitors. It was about $1,500 a month. On my first full day in town, I went out and spent $10,000 to furnish the place. Then I took possession of my car, which I'd had shipped from Toronto. By the end of the day, I was settled.

I then moved on to my next step: I needed a manager. I left messages for many of the big names: 3 Arts, Principato-Young and a handful of others. I also phoned George Shapiro, who was best known for managing the career of Jerry Seinfeld. We'd actually met for about thirty seconds in Aspen, when he came up to me, shook my hand and told me he'd enjoyed my set. As soon as he wandered off, another comic rushed up to me and said, "My God. Do you know who that was? That was George Shapiro." I had no idea.

Remembering that moment, I decided to call him. I left him a message. Two days later, the phone rang. Until that point in my life, I'd answered the phone by saying, "Hello?" In Los Angeles, I decided I'd say, "Gerry Dee here," thinking it was more professional.

"Hi, Gerry," said the voice on the other end of the line, "it's George Shapiro."

"Hello," I sputtered.

"Listen," he said, "I got your call. And yes, of course I remember you. I'm not really taking on any new clients, but I just wanted to phone and wish you the best of luck."

That was it. The phone call was over. I was the farthest thing from disappointed—George Shapiro had phoned *me*. It was the greatest rejection I had ever had.

By the end of the week, I got a return call from a manager named Barry Katz. I knew him because I'd opened a couple of times for Dane Cook, one of his biggest clients. He also represented Michael Richards—aka Cosmo Kramer on *Seinfeld*—and, for a time, had repped Dave Chappelle. We spoke briefly. I gave him the basic premise for a sitcom I had in mind. He agreed to take me on. The very next day, he called me.

"Gerry," he said in that thick Boston accent of his, "it's Barry. I got a job you might be interested in. *National Lampoon* is filming a special in which they get comics from around the world to perform. You know . . . sort of an *International Lampoon*? Anyway, they need a Canadian. The gig's yours if you want it. It pays five hundred dollars, but the exposure would be huge."

"Wait a minute," I said. "This is the same *National Lampoon* that did *Animal House* and those *Vacation* movies?"

"One and the same."

"Of course I'll do it."

"Good," he said. "I'll let them know."

We talked a little bit more. Apparently, he was already lining up networks to hear my pitch for my television show. I thanked him. The call lasted no more than five minutes. I took stock. I'd been in Los Angeles for exactly one week. In that time, I'd found an apartment, bought furniture, acquired a manager, booked a *National Lampoon* special and lined up pitch meetings for my television show. This, I thought, was *easy*. Why hadn't I done this earlier? I filmed the special; it was recorded at a club down by the beach. I quickly concluded that I was there to stay. I liked the weather. I started looking for a house to buy and a golf club to join.

My idea was called *Substitute Teacher*. It was actually more of a reality show, in which I'd play the worst teacher of all time. Here was the gag: the students would be real students, at a real school, and they'd have no idea that I was an actor. Hidden cameras, meanwhile, would record all the shenanigans. While we had no idea how this would possibly work—could we find a school that would allow it?—Barry and I assumed we'd figure it all out later. In the meantime, Barry got us into pitch meetings with the big four networks: CBS, ABC, NBC and Fox. He also managed to get us a meeting with Fremantle, a British production company that has aired television shows all over the globe.

We pitched over the course of six days, during which I learned a valuable lesson about the way things work in Hollywood: at every meeting you will ever have, you will feel like your idea is adored. You will leave the meeting feeling like it is a done deal. At one point, I said to Barry, "If more than one of them want the show, how do we know who to pick?" That's how naive I was.

Over the next two days, every network we'd pitched passed. We went back to the drawing board. I wrote a script for another idea I had. I didn't really know how to write a television script, so I bought a book on how to do it. I also wandered into Hollywood and found a store that sold actual scripts from famous shows and movies. I would read them and take notes. That's how I would learn.

My second idea was called *Head Coach*, and it was fairly similar to *Mr. D*, except that it took place in the world of minor hockey. Barry liked it as well. He contacted all of the execs who, quite recently, had shut the door on *Substitute Teacher*. We didn't get a single meeting. Note to self: don't pitch about hockey to anyone. It doesn't sell. Maybe in Canada, but even that's tough because they can't sell it internationally.

Oddly, I wasn't that disappointed. In a way, I'd tried to cheat the system a bit.

I really felt that, to get the ball rolling, I needed to get on *The Tonight Show* and then kill on *The Tonight Show*. There was one problem: getting on *The Tonight Show*. This was the LA system—no one cared about you as a comedian until you were a name, and you weren't a name until you did Carson or Leno or Letterman. Or you got lucky. Or you ground it out in LA (or New York) for a long, long time. And so, as our next line of attack, Barry set out to get me my shot on the biggest program on late-night television.

At the time, you had to impress a pair of talent bookers

named Bob Read and Ross Mark. It's not like Bob and Ross were funny people or comics themselves. They were, however, in charge of determining who was funny enough to appear on *The Tonight Show*. They decided who got on the air by conducting auditions—they called them "show-cases"—in which a few selected comics did four-to-five-minute sets in a local comedy club. If Bob and Ross liked any of them, they'd book them on the show. If not, they all went home.

Barry called Bob and Ross. Owing to my success in San Francisco, he got me a spot at a *Tonight Show* showcase, which was being held in the famous Hollywood Improv. It was a small crowd, with lots of good comics. Though I thought I'd done well, it was hard to say, since it wasn't a typical crowd, mostly filled with other comics and their respective managers and agents, and I knew that they weren't going to laugh at their competition. At the end of the day, Bob and Ross told me I wasn't ready. I went back a couple of weeks later. They told me again I wasn't ready. I went back again, and again, and again, performing alongside such comics as Ken Jeong, Judah Friedlander, Zach Galifianakis and Craig Robinson.

After my sixth showcase, Bob and Ross asked to talk to me.

"Gerry," they said, "you're ready."

"Thank you."

"We want to book you for the show."

"Really? That's fantastic. Thank you so much. Do you know when I'll do it?"

"No, but we'll figure it out and let Barry know."

I was elated. I'd been in Los Angeles close to a year and had been starting to feel like maybe, just maybe, I'd bitten off more than I could chew. Though my bank account hadn't quite run out, I was starting to dislike the fact that I wasn't making any money in the City of Angels. But no! My insecurity was just that—insecurity. I was a guy who'd just booked *The Tonight Show*. Millions of people would see me. If I did well, Barry would be able to get more agents, producers and networks interested in my career. I went home. I'm sure I celebrated that night.

I never did get a date given to me and then the bookers moved on from that role. To this day, I don't know why. Undeterred, Barry tried to get me on a Letterman showcase. No luck. I just wasn't good enough, I guess.

Did I give up then? No—I focused my attention on trying to become a regular at all the main comedy clubs in the Los Angeles area. Around this time, Barry Katz had assigned me to an underling who had stopped returning my calls. So, even though I had a manager—at least on paper—I began to feel like I was very much on my own. I arranged all my gigs myself.

I started making calls. I played every room I could. I played the Comedy Magic Club and the Icehouse, both of which were on the outskirts of Los Angeles. I played Tuesday nights at a restaurant called Dublin's. I played at a coffee shop in Venice Beach. I played at an Asian restaurant in Hollywood. I did a basement on La Brea. I even managed to get a five-minute spot once every six weeks at the Hollywood Improv. Most of the rooms I played were run by other comics. The audience—if, indeed, there was one—was made up of the comics who were performing that night, along with their families and friends. Few laughed at anyone else. Playing into this void, I began to feel like I was getting worse, not better. Plus, I really was starting to run out of money. And so I would literally have to leave LA to generate any income. I'd either go back to Canada to play some clubs or do a US college or two. It was a strange existence: living in LA but mostly making my money outside of the city. And when I *was* in LA, it was back to the grind of doing these five-minute sets to try to get noticed at the clubs.

Finally, I got the call. I could showcase for Mitzi Shore, the owner of the Comedy Store (and mother of Pauly Shore). The Comedy Store was the most iconic comedy club in Los Angeles. Outside, you could sign the wall once you were made a regular. Name a famous comic, and they have signed that wall. And to be made a regular, you needed to be approved by one person, and one person only: Mitzi. Again, the rule was hard and fast. If she liked you, you were in. If not, you weren't ready and would have to try again until she thought you were. I got three minutes on a Wednesday night. I was the ninth comic of fifteen. Mitzi was in her seventies, and in poor health—I remember watching someone help her to the table where she sat at the back of the room. One by one, the other comics went on. Mitzi, who was famously hard to impress, rarely laughed. During the eighth comic's set, I noticed that one of the doormen stopped by Mitzi's table. She leaned over to talk to him. Just as the eighth comic finished his set, she struggled to her feet and left with the doorman. I went on anyway. She never came back that night. I never became a regular at the Comedy Store, and I never signed that wall.

I did manage to get booked on *The Late, Late Show*, which was hosted by Craig Kilborn. Though it wasn't Leno or Letterman, it was still a late-night talk show, and if I did well, my appearance just might generate enough heat to resuscitate my plans for a sitcom. In other words, I had a lot riding on my appearance. I'd never been so nervous. Halfway through my first minute in front of a US national audience, I got such a bad case of dry mouth that I found it difficult to move my lips. Still, I mustered the face and cheek muscle strength to plow through a very average set. The show was taped in the afternoon. I remember watching it that night in a bar, thinking, *You bombed. You went out there and bombed. That's what you did.*

After things didn't pan out at the Comedy Store, I was left with one last option among the big Hollywood clubs: while the Laugh Factory on Sunset Boulevard wasn't quite as influential as the Comedy Store, it ran a close second. I was able to get a spot through my new manager, Brian. By this point, I was out of disposable income, tired of the LA grind, disappointed that having a manager was no guarantee of success and lonely. I was beyond caring, in other words. As I waited for my six-minute set, I decided, right then and there, that I was going to destroy that night.

Three hours earlier, I had bombed on Kilborn, and to be honest, I was pissed. And true to my vow, I killed that night—ironically, doing the exact same set I had done on

Kilborn. But this time, with no dry mouth, just "fed-up" mouth.

When it was over, we all waited in a line to meet the owner of the club, Jamie Masada. That was the way it worked: you'd walk up to a table where he was sitting, and he would tell you whether you were in or out. When it was my turn, I shook his hand.

"You were very funny," he said in his thick Persian accent.

"Thank you."

"You have a manager?" he asked. Jamie also managed comics, so if he liked what he saw at this showcase and you didn't have one, he might take you on as a client.

"I do," I told him. He paused.

"Okay, I like you. Very funny tonight. Come back in six months and do ten minutes."

I was stunned. "I killed tonight doing six minutes, and you want me to come back in six months to do an extra four minutes?"

"Yes. You were very funny. Come back, six months. For ten minutes, yes?"

"I don't think I want to do that," I told him, "but thanks anyway."

I left and walked out. I had failed to become a regular at any of the big clubs.

Two days later, I received an email from Brian in which he informed me that he and Barry would be parting ways with me. "Parting ways" is a nice way to say "You aren't making us any money, so we are letting you go." He wasn't wrong. I knew it was over anyway. Brian hadn't responded to me in months, and to be honest, I think he just knew there was nothing left he could do. As frustrating as it was, I knew there was no point for him to keep managing me. You can't sell what people ain't buying, and they weren't buying Gerry Dee in Hollywood.

I sent Barry an email:

> Hey, Barry,
> I just received Brian's email that you will no longer be representing me. I know this is not how either of us planned on this working out, but I just wanted to thank you for your efforts. I wish you the best moving forward.
>
> —Gerry

He responded immediately: "You're a class act. Take care."

So, what did I do? I found someone to take over my apartment lease until it ended. I sold all of my furniture, shipped my car back to Toronto and went home. I suppose I'd had a bit of an epiphany: if making it in Los Angeles was the only way to truly succeed, then maybe I didn't want to succeed that badly. But then I had another thought: maybe there was another way to do it, one that didn't involve the Comedy Store/*Tonight Show*/sitcom conveyor belt. Maybe I could go home to Canada and blow up there, so much so that if I ever did decide to return to Los Angeles, it was only because the city had invited me.

So that's what I did. I started doing theatres again. Soon after, I landed a role on a CBC miniseries playing Wayne

Cashman in the remake of the 1972 Canada–Russia hockey series. That led to an audition for *Trailer Park Boys: The Movie*. I was up for the role of Donny, a prison guard who has a fractious relationship with the character known as Ricky. In the audition scene, Ricky yells, "Suck it, Donny!" at my character. The scripted line I was supposed to say was "*You* suck it." But in my audition, I added the word *more*—"You suck it, more!" Later, Mike Volpe, one of the producers, would tell me that adding that single word cracked everyone up, including Ivan Reitman, who was also a producer. Imagine, the word *more* got me my first feature film role.

One night, a few years later, I found myself doing a gig at a two-thousand-seat Calgary venue called Jack Singer Hall. After the show, I was visited in my dressing room by none other than Barry Katz, who happened to be in the city with Dane Cook, who was appearing that same night at the Scotiabank Saddledome.

"Congratulations on your success," he said.

"Thank you."

"Gerry," he told me, "if you're amenable, I'd like to rep you in the States again."

I thought about it for a moment. Finally, I said: "Okay, Barry, if we do this, it can't be like before. You guys can't ignore my emails. You can't ignore my calls. You can't ignore my texts."

He agreed.

So he started managing me in the States again. Little changed. I still had trouble getting him on the phone, and

I was turning down a lot of the gigs he *was* getting me. One day, I sent him an email informing him that it might be best if we "parted company." He responded by wishing me the best of luck in the future. Barry was a good guy.

In 2022, I was invited to perform as part of the Netflix Is a Joke comedy festival. My set was at the Laugh Factory. My name was on the billboard. The crowd was small, as Dave Chappelle was performing down the street. I did okay. Just okay. I couldn't wait to get home.

I don't miss Los Angeles at all.

# YOU'RE NOT FAMOUS

If I had to identify the cornerstone of my personality—the one thing that makes me *me*—I'd have to say it's this: when I get an idea in my head, I not only *have* to make it happen, I have to make it happen immediately. The other day, my youngest daughter told me she thought she might like to pursue volleyball more. Within an hour, I'd signed her up for an elite volleyball camp. When my son found an old guitar in the basement and said he might like to learn how to play it, I immediately downloaded an app that promised mastery in just three short months. (It cost $139. He used it for two days.) The other day, my wife, Heather, told me she had her eye on something called the Dyson Airwrap curling iron. That afternoon, I went to the mall and tried to find her one, even though she'd warned me they were sold out everywhere. I would eventually find it. I like to please people, especially my family. Sometimes, this backfires.

Is there a name for this condition? I suppose I could be described as impulsive, except that there's a twist. Lots of impulsive people get an idea and start to follow through, only to get sidetracked by another idea, at which point they give up on the first one. This never happens to me. I'm saddled with a compulsion to see my latest idea through to the end, and it doesn't matter whether it's likely to be good, horrible or somewhere in the middle. I just can't seem to tell the difference until it's all over. This condition, this compulsive-impulsivity, has at times done right by me. The day after I got the idea for a television show, I started pitching it to anybody who would listen. Without this determination, *Mr. D* would never have gotten on the air.

But then, there are those other times.

One day in the fall of 2008, I got a message via my website from a fan. I think his name was Jim, or John, or maybe Jack. He asked if I might be playing Sudbury when my new DVD came out. Working comics often get mail like this—people who like your act and want you to come to their hometowns so they can see you perform and perhaps meet you after a show. Most comics either answer the email or they don't, and it all ends there. In my case, this innocent message gave birth to one of my obsessive-impulsive notions, an idea bolstered by the fact that, a few days earlier, I'd seen Russell Peters signing copies of his new DVD, *Red, White and Brown*, at a local record store. It was an impressive sight. People were lined up outside the store to meet him. As Jim (or John, or maybe Jack) had reminded me, *I* had a new DVD coming out. This, I thought, could be an opportunity.

46

I was, however, failing to recognize an important distinction between Russell Peters and me. In 2008, Russell played back-to-back shows at the Air Canada Centre. I'm not talking about a small bowl of seats carved out of the ACC—he filled the whole arena, both nights, just him and a microphone at one end, with twenty thousand fans or more watching at the other. My DVD, *No Reading Ahead*, had been performed at the Joseph Workman Auditorium, a two-hundred-seat venue that operated within a Toronto psychiatric hospital called the Centre for Addiction and Mental Health. Another key difference? At my gig, about a third of the seats were empty, even though the tickets were free. Though I knew I wouldn't create the same lineups that Peters had generated at his signing—that would be unrealistic!—I still felt that, given my relative success, I could pull two or three hundred per signing, as I had grown a bit in stature since the DVD was released.

So I phoned the head office of HMV. I was connected to a promotions manager named Lawrence who, through some monumental fluke, happened to be a fan of mine. I told him my idea: with a new DVD coming out, I could host signings at HMVs in the cities where I had upcoming tour dates—namely, Peterborough, London, Calgary, Edmonton, Hamilton and St. John's. Lawrence loved the idea. "Don't worry," I remember him saying, "I'll take care of everything."

Four months later, I found myself driving to Peterborough for my first signing. It was a beautiful autumn day, and the leaves were beginning to turn colour. I couldn't enjoy it, though. The mind, when nervous, leapfrogs between best-case and worst-case scenarios, and mine was no exception. One second, I'd imagine an empty record store. A second later, I'd picture a lineup extending from the front entrance of the mall, only to wrap around the adjoining garden centre, so as to not interfere with traffic. Yet my rational mind—that small part of my brain that was, in some small way, connected to reality—still held to what I'd initially imagined. There'd be two or three hundred fans, money in hand, wanting a handshake, an autograph and a brief chat. And so, as I drove, I thought of how far I had come in the seven years since I first started stand-up comedy: all those awful gigs, all that lonely practice, all those grinding road trips, all the bad food and lumpy hotel mattresses.

When I got to Peterborough, I pulled over at a Staples and bought a half-dozen Sharpies, just in case Lawrence had forgotten to bring some—or in case the ones he had brought dried after repeated use. As I approached the mall, I wondered whether I should park in the back, so as not to run into any of the fans coming in through the front. I did this, just to be safe. The signing was at one o'clock. I was deliberately late by a few minutes. It's an old night-club trick—force people to line up outside, even though the club is empty inside, the thinking being that passersby will be attracted by the crowds. I was a marketing genius, in my mind.

I entered the mall. My heart was racing, for it suddenly seemed so impossibly exciting that people would come out not to see me perform, but to simply meet *me*, the man behind the microphone. I reached the store and immediately saw what Lawrence meant by taking care of everything. There was a huge banner bearing my photograph and the words "Gerry Dee Live At HMV Autograph Meet and Greet DVD Signing Tour." It stretched over a pair of six-foot tables, which had been placed end to end and covered with a single cloth. This created a twelve-foot-long counter upon which the store manager had stacked about two hundred copies of my DVD (as well as, I noticed, a half-dozen Sharpies). Meanwhile, the table was flanked by a pair of unsmiling security guards who had been hired to control the crowds in the event that they became unruly. Good thinking, Lawrence. The last thing I needed was some type of stampede of people trying to get to me.

Lawrence was there, too. He had driven all the way from Toronto. He was in his late twenties. He was wearing slacks and a blue HMV polo. I shook his hand. If he seemed sheepish, it was for a very good reason: exactly three people were in line. I tried not to panic. Instead, I chatted with Lawrence. This tactic, I hoped, would allow more fans to arrive, lengthen the line a little and create the people-attracting atmosphere known as a buzz. Lawrence and I gabbed about the traffic on the way up (it was fine), about whether we had trouble finding the place (we hadn't), about whether either one of us knew Peterborough well (no, not really). Around one thirty, it occurred to Lawrence that, should we keep the three people waiting any longer, they might leave, our stalling tactic having accomplished nothing beyond obliterating the tiny lineup that we *did* have.

"I think we should get started," he said.

"Good idea," I responded.

My first fan was tall and thin and wore glasses; she looked about thirteen years of age. She giggled nervously as she approached. A middle-aged man, obviously her father, stood to one side. I decided that I'd engage her in conversation, if only to create more time for latecomers to join the line.

"Hi!" I said. "What's your name?"

"Elizabeth."

"Hi, Elizabeth. You in school?"

"Yes."

"Where do you go?"

"Immaculate Conception Catholic School."

"Oh. Do you play sports?"

"Not really."

This was not the answer I was hoping for. I can talk sports with anybody, for any amount of time, no matter where I am.

"Is there anything you want to ask me about?"

"Not really," she said.

There was an uncomfortable pause. I was looking at her, and she was looking at me, and the only thing I could think to do was suggest a question she might want to ask me, even though she had plainly stated that she really didn't want to. "How's about 'What's it like doing stand-up?'"

"Uh, okay . . ."

I launched into a spiel about travelling the country and making people laugh, and while it wasn't all fun and games—oh no, Elizabeth, like anything that's worth doing, it's a lot of hard work and frustration, and don't get me *started* about the food on the road, all those truck stops and fast-food joints—I have to say there's nothing I'd rather be doing than comedy. On and on I went, describing a life she had no intention of ever pursuing, until finally I ended my monologue with a line so pandering that, all these years later, it still makes me shudder. "But the best part," I told her, "is getting to meet fans like you."

What did Elizabeth do? How did this innocent thirteen-year-old from Peterborough respond? She blinked, turned her head and looked at the lineup. In the time we'd been talking, the second person had grown tired of waiting and left. It was now her and the man behind her. She then turned back toward me.

"Can you sign my DVD?" she asked. "I really have to go."

So I did. I took my time, writing: *To Elizabeth, from Immaculate Conception Catholic School in Peterborough, good luck in school and thanks for coming and meeting me today. Hope you enjoy the rest of your day.—Gerry Dee.*

She looked at it with a puzzled expression, then walked away with her father, who seemed even more impatient than she did. I turned to one of the security guards.

"Chatty little thing," I said.

By this point, I'd admitted to myself that this whole signing was a disaster, one that would leave everyone involved in a state of extreme humiliation. It was a list that included me, Lawrence and the nameless store manager, who, in a very short period of time, would be restocking all but two of the two hundred DVDs he had placed on my oversized, police-protected signing table. And so I changed my strategy. I would quickly sign the other fan's DVD, mumble a few words of thanks and get the hell out.

Yet I was up against a steel-fastened truth in the entertainment industry. While people in an autograph lineup will generally be, at the very least, veering toward normality, the last person will seem slightly off. This adage holds true, no matter whether the line is two thousand or two. He (or she) will purposefully anchor the line so that, when his (or her) time finally comes, there's no reason to end the conversation. On this day, his name was Michael. After saying hello, he started the conversation with a statement that never fails to cause chills to run down the spine of a professional comic.

"You know," he said, "I've always wanted to be a comic. Everyone says I'm really funny."

Then the questions started. "How do you get started in the business? Do you have a manager? How do you get on TV? How much do you make when you first start out?"

Ironically, I'd already answered most of his questions during the endless monologue I'd directed at poor Elizabeth; if he'd listened in, none of this pointless *blah-blah-blah* would've been necessary. When he finally left, I once again turned to the security guard stationed nearest me and asked, "Why didn't you move him along?"

"I didn't think you wanted me to," he said. "I mean, you spent so much time with your other fan."

There it was. *Fan*. Never has a word so wounded, simply because it had been used in the singular.

Lawrence came over and took mercy on me: "I think we can probably wrap this up."

"Sorry about that," I said.

"I thought it would go better. You know, it's probably because the Petes were playing this afternoon as well."

"Yes!" I said. "Junior hockey is really big in smaller markets! I bet you're right, Lawrence. I bet you're right."

London, the location of my next appearance, was a week away. Lawrence and I both checked that the city's hockey team, the London Knights, weren't playing the same afternoon as the Gerry Dee Live at HMV Autograph Meet and Greet DVD Signing Tour. It wasn't. Could this really make a difference? London was a bigger market. You never knew. I didn't need any more Sharpies, so I drove straight to the event. Once again, Lawrence met me at the front of the store. The banner was still there, though the signing table was much smaller, there weren't nearly as many DVDs for sale and there was only one security guard.

Lawrence and I looked awkwardly at one another, neither of us mentioning a glaring, obvious fact: no one had come. *No one.* I sat in my seat and spun a Sharpie on my thumb, like some high school student who didn't know the answer to a test question. After a while, I got up and wandered through the mall, hoping that someone—and by someone, I mean *anyone*—might recognize me and say, "Hey! Aren't you Gerry Dee?" At which point I'd shrug and say, "Why, yes I am! As a matter of fact, I'm at HMV right now, signing copies of my hilarious, new, shot-live-at-a-psychiatric-institution DVD. Why don't you drop by?"

We shut it down after an hour. Not a single person had come by. Lawrence, I noticed, was starting to find it difficult to look me in the eye. Yet he did tell me, with a sort of forced optimism in his voice, "I've got everything arranged at the next four cities."

In Calgary, I had a small, clothless table. There were ten DVDs, a single Sharpie and no security guard. No one came. Edmonton was a duplicate of Calgary. By the time I got to Hamilton, they had put me in a corner, behind a little table that was as big around as a large pizza. There was no banner and I didn't get a chair. The only interaction occurred when some guy wandered up to me and, thinking I worked at the store, asked, "Could you tell me where the jazz section is?"

I had one more city left—St. John's, Newfoundland. It would be a long flight. I'd have to leave the night before the event, and I had no earthly reason to suspect that even a single person might show up. And so I phoned the store and talked to a croaky-voiced adolescent who seemed completely unaware of the event. I told him I was too sick to come. Then I coughed.

"Uh, okay," he said.

I never spoke to Lawrence again. I hope he's doing well. Elizabeth is somewhere out there; I wonder if she still has the DVD with my essay-length signature. As for Michael, he still comes to my shows when I'm in Peterborough. Afterward, he waits for me outside the backstage door to get a photo. I always make as much time for him as he wants—if my DVD signing did anything, it made me appreciate that the Michaels of the world exist, and that I should never, ever take them for granted.

As for HMV, it closed for good in 2017. It is my sincere hope that I had nothing to do with this.

# WHEN CELEBRITIES GOLF

If you're a real celebrity, you get recognized by name. That's the benchmark. If you happen to be, say, Will Ferrell, and you're at the local mall, you will hear people saying, "Oh my God, isn't that Will Ferrell over there?" If you're Steve Carrell, and you take your car into the shop, the mechanic will look at you, grow a little wide-eyed and say, "*Damn*. Ain't you Steve Carrell?"

It's different for a Canadian celebrity. Let's say I'm in the grocery store, picking out apples for my kids, which they will later refuse to eat. On the rare occasion when I do get recognized, people manage some variation of "Hey, aren't you that guy from that show? You *know* the one I mean?" If they do know my name, they fumble it. I become Gary Deans, or Gerry Deeds, or Jimmy Dee. In return, I nod and try to be gracious. "Yes," I say. "I'm Gary Deans. It's nice to meet you." One day, I was walking on the boardwalk with my daughters when a group of ladies asked me if I would mind taking a picture. I assumed they meant *with* me, not *by* me. I tried to snuggle my way into the middle of the group until I got a death stare from one of them. "We don't want you in the picture," she said. Fair enough. They had no idea who Jimmy Dee was.

As a Canadian celebrity, I don't have an assistant, I don't have a publicist, I don't have a personal trainer and I certainly don't have any security. I travel to most of my events alone. As much as I would love to have my own entourage, a decent-sized touring group costs money I don't have. Plus, it'd look silly. If you stabbed Brad Pitt, it'd make the front page of the *New York Times*. But if I got hit over the head with a blunt object? That's a Twitter post, at best.

So, that means I travel alone, eat alone and answer my own emails. I do get them, by the way. They come through my website. Generally, they start with "I'm not sure if this email will ever get to you . . ." Of course it got to me; I'm reading it. It's understandable, really, as the general public doesn't understand another key difference between an American celebrity and a Canadian one: first of all, American celebrities are just called "celebrities," and second, "celebrities" aren't accessible. They can't be. It'd be dangerous, and they wouldn't get any work done. Canadian celebrities, on the other hand, *are* reachable. Sometimes, they're a little too accessible.

I once got an email from a fan who had bought tickets for the show I was about to do in Toronto.

"Hello Gerry," he wrote. "I recently purchased tickets for your upcoming concert. However, I forgot I have a friend's fiftieth birthday party to go to. Could you please refund my tickets?"

The easiest thing I could have done was ignore his request. Unfortunately, as a Canadian celebrity, I'm flattered when anyone writes to me, even if it's to ask for a refund, so I responded.

"Dear sir," I wrote. "I am sorry that you cannot attend the show but unfortunately, we don't refund tickets when people have conflicts. Perhaps you can give the tickets to someone who can use them? Thanks so much—Gerry Dee."

I thought that would be the end of it. I was wrong. He wrote me back, saying, "Seriously? How hard is it to apply a refund? You have my credit card, just reverse the charges." He obviously thought that, sitting beside me, was a spreadsheet or accounting system that had a copy of the credit card numbers of everybody who bought tickets to my tour.

At this point, I should have definitely stopped responding. I didn't.

"Hey, it's not really about out how easy or how hard it is to refund the tickets. It's that it's not something we do when people find they can't attend the shows after they've purchased a ticket. I'm sorry you can no longer attend, but perhaps you could give the tickets to someone who can . . . or sell them."

"Why should *I* sell them?" he responded. "It's your show! Can't you just sell the tickets on Kijiji for me?"

I wrote him back one more time, offering him tickets to another show. As I did, an uncomfortable thought started running through my head: *Would an actual celebrity,*

*Canadian or otherwise, actually do this?* This was quickly followed by yet another worry: *Maybe, Mr. Dee, you aren't the celebrity you thought you were.*

A case in point: In 2005, I got a call from a booking agency, asking if I'd come to a big corporate celebrity golf tournament. Michael Burgess from *The Phantom of the Opera* had pulled out at the last minute, and I suppose they were desperate for another celebrity player. I was more than a little surprised. At the time, I was just a comedian working the club circuit. Then again, I *was* starting to make a name for myself. Did this qualify me as a celebrity? I didn't think so. Still, you don't get asked to be a celebrity at a golf tournament if you aren't one. More importantly, they were also going to pay me a thousand dollars—not to perform, but to play golf, which I figured was another indication that my career had taken a turn toward celebrityhood.

So I said yes. On the day in question—it was beautiful and sunny, a gorgeous day to play golf—I drove, by myself, to the Bond Head golf course in Beeton, Ontario, a small town just north of Toronto. I wasn't surprised when no one greeted me. I'd come early, and I understood that I was a last-minute celebrity, the sort you only call at the very last minute when everyone else has said no.

I put my bag down and went to the registration table. It was staffed by a girl who looked about fourteen years of age. She wore a name tag reading *Tara*. She looked up at me, blinking.

"Hi," I said. "Is this where I check in?"

"Yes, sir. Your name?"

"Gerry Dee."

She checked a list in front of her, her eyes moving down the page, and then up the page, and then down the page once more.

"Uhhh . . . Could you spell that for me?"

"G-E-R-R-Y," I said.

"Hmm . . . and your last name?" she asked.

I paused. "D-E-E."

She looked some more, her eyes narrowed. At the same time, I tried to sound helpful instead of desperate. "Maybe," I offered, "you should check the back of the page."

She slowly looked up, lowered her chin and raised her eyebrows, like you do when speaking with an idiot. I'd never seen such a condescending look, and it didn't help that it was coming from a girl wearing braces. "Look," I said, "I'm supposed to be here, so maybe you can ask someone?"

She wandered off. I waited at the table, hoping someone might legitimize my presence by recognizing me and asking me for an autograph or photo. This did not happen. Tara came back with a middle-aged woman in pleated shorts and a polo shirt.

"Hi," she said.

"Hi," I said.

We stood looking at each other. I was frowning. She looked confused. "I'm one of the celebrities," I told her.

"Oh! What's your name?"

"Gerry Dee."

"Let me just have a quick . . ." She took the sign-up sheet. Now *her* eyes were travelling up and down the list. "Hmm.

Well, we don't have you here—I believe Tara may have mentioned that—but don't worry, you're here now. Let's get you set up."

She asked one of the staff to take my clubs and throw them on a cart that, I noticed, bore a label reading *Michael Burgess*.

This, I should have known, was not a good sign.

If you're not a golfer, or have never been to a celebrity golf tournament, it works this way: people pay money to have a famous person in their foursome, and that money goes to charity.

As I was early, I figured I'd go hit some balls. This, I thought, would accomplish two things. First, it'd give me something to do. Second, it'd let the threesome who had drawn me as their celebrity see me play. This way, even if they didn't know me, they'd be pleased with the fact that, famous or not, I was at least a good golfer. I'd been playing since I was twelve, and it was not uncommon for me, as a teenager, to play over a hundred rounds of golf during the summer. In 1986, I went to the Canadian Junior Golf Championship in Edmonton, where I placed forty-ninth. (Mike Weir placed seventh.) I even owned a golf bag that Callaway, the golf equipment company, had made especially for me. In hindsight, it looked stupid; it was a tour-sized bag, and it did make people think I was either a professional or some idiot who *thought* he was a professional.

After hitting a few balls and not getting recognized once, I decided to go putt. As the putting green started to become more crowded, I started to recognize a lot of celebrities. Wendel Clark was there, as were Darryl Sittler and Tom

Cochrane. And while they all seemed to know each other, none of them knew me. This, I have to admit, was not a good feeling. So, I hit a few more putts and returned to my cart, where I hoped I'd finally meet the threesome who'd be golfing with me. There was a problem, though: I wasn't in their group anymore. When I got to the cart, my Callaway tour bag was gone. Did someone steal it? I found the organizer and told her my problem. She looked uncomfortable.

"It wasn't stolen," she told me.

"It wasn't?"

"No, it wasn't." She took a slight breath. "It's just that . . . well . . . Your threesome asked if they could play with someone whom they . . . uh . . . as they put it . . . had *heard* of. But don't worry, we'll find it." I told her it had my name on it. She fake-smiled and left.

I started looking. There were about seventy carts in all. As I searched, I still had my putter in my hand. After looking for about ten minutes, I finally did find the Callaway bag with my name on it, sitting on a distant cart. I was about to put my putter into my bag when a staff member came up and unloaded my bag, explaining that my second threesome had rejected me as well. If anyone hadn't seen the bag when I arrived, they were seeing it now, as it was being passed around from group to group like the worst kid at recess when you picked teams. By this point, the bag was more famous than I was.

A sort of survival instinct came over me—the same type that kicks in when you're performing for a near-empty club, and you're bombing, and you have to yell to be heard over the ceiling fan. *Just do the gig,* spoke a little voice in my head. *Then get your cheque and get out.*

In the end, they put me in a cart that was short a participant, meaning that the pair of golfers who did show up now had the privilege of playing with not one but two celebrities: myself, and former NHLer Mike Gartner. We all introduced ourselves. They both knew who Mike Gartner was. Neither of them knew who I was, as became painfully obvious on our first hole. It was a par three. In these types of events, on par-three holes the closest to the pin wins a prize. Naturally, this doesn't apply to the celebrity (or, in our case, the *celebrities*). I hit my 8 iron about eight feet from the pin, making my shot the closest in our group.

The others congratulated me and handed me the closest-to-the-pin sheet—which, as a celebrity, I was not supposed to sign. Yet it would have been embarrassing to admit that I was *supposed* to be their celebrity, which didn't even make sense, since they already had one. "Nice job, Gerry!" one of them said. "Write your name down!"

"Oh, that's okay," I said. "I'm not here to win prizes."

Mike Gartner weighed in. "Go on, Gerry. Get your name on there! I can't win anything, but *you guys* sure can."

So, there it was. The other celebrity didn't know me, either. Grimacing, I pretended to put my name down, and off we went. As the match went on, I began to relax. It was a great day, and, if you removed my ego from the equation, there was no denying that, whatever else, I was still getting paid to play golf. By the fifteenth hole, I was even starting to look forward to the dinner that would follow.

Then, it finally happened. Two guys driving by from a different group slammed on the brakes as they passed us on the tee block.

"Gerry Dee?" they shouted. Everyone in our group was stunned, including me. "Can we get a picture?"

"Of course," I said, trying to contain the joy in my head, a joy that validated why I had a tour bag with my name on it in huge letters. They asked Mike Gartner to take the photo, which he was happy to do, if a little confused. The two twentysomethings drove off. I don't know how they knew me, nor did I care. The bottom line was that it explained a lot to the group. In fact, I hoped word would get back to Tara, the Grade 9 girl at the registration table who clearly didn't believe that I had any right to be there.

After golf, we had dinner, where the speaker was a former NHL player who travels the country performing at events like this. I ate chicken with my fellow golfers. Shortly after we were done, a person from the agency that had booked me for the event started handing out envelopes to the celebrities in attendance. I figured they were the appearance fees. When it became obvious that he didn't have one for me, I was faced with the humbling prospect of wondering if they had mine.

"Do you have an envelope for me?" I asked.

"And your name is?" he asked.

"I'm Gerry Dee."

"And you're one of the celebrities? I don't have you on my list."

"Yeah, I was added late, but don't worry, I can get it later."

"Wait here," he said. "I'll go and see if I can figure this out."

I waited and waited. Everyone was starting to leave, so I grabbed a seat near the front entrance. The head of the agency appeared, seemingly out of nowhere. Weirdly, he knelt down in front of the chair in which I was sitting.

"I'm sorry," he said. "I didn't realize you were coming. I don't have a cheque for you, but if you give me your address, I'll send it as soon as possible."

"No big deal," I said. I meant it, too: I totally understood that I was a last-minute addition, and I knew that I didn't fall under the category of "celebrity," even though they had brought me in as one. It was a conversation I wished I'd had during that first phone call. "I'll come," I should've said, "but just a heads-up: I really don't see myself as a celebrity."

I waited a few weeks. The cheque never came. I emailed the agency and was told it would be sent that week. I waited another two weeks, then called and left a message on the machine. The head of the agency, the same guy who had knelt before me, called me back and told me he'd send the money right away. A little later, I thought I'd call him one more time to see if I could track down this thousand dollars he owed me. He picked up the phone and said, "Look, you'll get your money, but let's be honest, you're not a celebrity." I remember how much that killed me. He was right, but the embarrassment of actually being told that stung.

But, I explained to him, someone from his agency had reached out to me and asked me to be there. "I'm not on the phone to debate if I'm a celebrity or not," I told him. "I just want the money I'm owed." In a childish, yet confident manner, I then stated, "And maybe one day I *will* be a celebrity."

I could hear him laugh after I said that.

He eventually sent the money. The thousand dollars was definitely not worth all of this humiliation. But my time would come to get my just deserts. Ironically, it would happen *during* dessert.

Fast-forward ten years. My career had taken off, and I got a call to entertain the crowd at a charity event, the Rogers Conn Smythe Sports Celebrity Dinner and Auction. I was at the head table with a who's who of people from the Canadian sports and entertainment industry. When it was time for dessert, I went up to perform. That's when I recognized the owner of the agency, sitting at table four. So I did what any comedian would do: I told the story of his hiring me ten years earlier, ending with his telling me, "Let's be honest, you're not a celebrity." I had to. I didn't *need* to, but in my mind, I *had* to. To his credit, he came up to me afterward and said, "I totally deserved that."

We now laugh about it. He reaches out once in a while to see if I can do an event for him; if I'm not busy, I'll actually say yes. And why not? That's my level of celebrity. I still answer my own emails, return my own phone calls and drive myself to my own gigs. But, every time he hires me, I make him hold up a sign as I perform that says, "Gerry Dee is a celebrity." I'm kidding. I don't do that. But it'd be funny.

And yes, I still have a Callaway tour bag with my name on it, but I don't dare use it.

# PART TWO

The Road to *Mr. D*

# THE WORLD-FAMOUS IMPROV

'd been a working comic for about three years when I met the booker for the Improv Comedy Club in Tempe, Arizona. The Improv was a chain of comedy clubs across the US, and they were good clubs. They were also big. I had never booked a weekend at an American comedy club, and I knew that if I could get my foot in the door at one of the Improvs, I could perhaps get into more of them. Though I forget the booker's name, she ended up getting me a weekend as the MC in Tempe. I was pumped; they were paying me five hundred dollars for five shows over three nights—though I really wasn't doing it for the money.

MCs at comedy clubs aren't typically the strongest act on the show. A three-person show would have an MC, a middle or feature act, and then the headliner. An MC and a middle aren't supposed to do better than the headliner, but it does happen. And in this case, I felt this was exactly what was going to happen. I didn't know who the other two comics were, and I didn't care. I figured they didn't know it yet, but they would have a tough time following "Gerry Dee, the headliner from Canada"—especially the headliner. In fact, I kind of felt bad for him.

I flew down with my friend Steve Mason. We'd golf a few rounds, have a few drinks and then watch me destroy onstage every night. We arrived at the club. I saw the headliner's name on the marquee. The middle's name was below his. Mine was not mentioned. *That's okay*, I thought. *The club will feel stupid when I blow the other two off the stage.*

I met the staff and got my instructions for the night, mostly housekeeping stuff for when I got onstage. The anticipation was killing me. The place was packed. I had never seen so many people in a comedy club. I was going to kill with such a big crowd. I remember seeing people with signs in the crowd. I'd never seen that in Canada. They treated their comedy like a sporting event. *I guess that's how they do it in America*, I thought. Maybe they would whip up some signs for me for the following night?

Just before the show, the headliner came up to me and introduced himself. Then he gave me a bunch of things he wanted me to say about him. Something about his book, something about a movie he was going to be in, something about another TV appearance. He mentioned dates, co-stars, titles and more. I tuned it all out. Normally, headliners give the MC one or two things to say, not ten. I knew I was going to forget most of it by the time I brought him onstage forty minutes later. Besides, after seeing me, the audience wasn't going to remember him anyway.

The show was about to start. Steve was in the back. Earlier, he'd been pumping me up: "You're going to kill in here. This crowd is amazing." Then the voice of God came over the speakers. "Hey, everyone, please welcome to the stage, Gerry Dee." There was a smattering of applause. *That's okay*, I thought. *That'll change.*

Or so I thought. I did okay. Just okay. What the hell? I usually did really well with the bits I went with that night— all my good bits. I was a tad more nervous because the stakes were so high, but I really did expect I'd do a lot better. After each bit, I was a little confused as to why they weren't killing the way they had done before.

Then I introduced the next act.

"Please welcome . . . Gary Gulman."

Gulman was a young comic from New York via Massachusetts. He did really well. I mean, *really* well—so funny, so polished. I was surprised by how good he was because I'd never heard of him.

After Gary was finished, I went back up and did another ten minutes of average comedy about my parents being Scottish or the last wedding I went to. Then it was headliner time. Though the guy had given me ten things to say, at that point I was mostly trying to remember his name. I mentioned one or two of the things, then I saw him pacing beside the stage. He was eager to get on. So I finally brought him up.

"Please welcome . . . Dane Cook!"

The place went ballistic. People started cheering and yelling and whistling. Women were trying to touch him, and all those signs—all of those *We Love You, Dane* placards—were thrust toward the ceiling, the sign holders on their feet, just like everyone else in the erupting room. Finally, the audience settled down. It took him two full minutes to quiet them. Then he went for an hour or more and destroyed. Like, I mean *destroyed*. I had never seen anything like this, and it would be years before I would see it again. It was like a rock concert. I slouched in my seat at the back. I had never been so humbled. They were all there to see *him*. These were his fans, and he had a lot of them. It was the difference between a crowd watching a known person versus an unknown. I was beyond impressed.

After the show, he signed stuff, sold merchandise and took photos for another hour. This was also new to me. Meanwhile, I just stood there. Not one person came up to me. Not one.

I'd never seen anyone so confidently sell his material, his movements so electric that, in a very short period of time, I began to think it wasn't so much the material that made Dane Cook so popular, but the highly individualistic way he punched it up. It was a sickening moment. Suddenly, I realized I wasn't very good. Jerry Seinfeld is famous for saying, "Years in comedy are like years in life. If you've been a comic for twenty years, you're as good in comedy as a twenty-year-old is in life." As a comic, I was an infant. I could toddle, and I could spit up on my shirt front. That was about it. I knew that, now, and it was all thanks to Dane

Cook. I also realized that I came from a very small scene, a.k.a. Canada, and that to get better, I'd have to break out of the little world in which I lived—namely the ten clubs or so that I played in north of the border.

I did a little research and found out that Cook was very active on social media, which was just beginning back then—he was the first comic I knew who had a MySpace account, and who responded to direct messages and emails. And before long, he blew up: there were sold-out shows at Madison Square Garden, major talk show appearances, movie roles, and best-selling DVDs.

Soon after my appearance in Tempe, I moved to Los Angeles. There, I began to appear at a club on Sunset Strip called Dublin's—by "appear," I mean that I'd go on whenever they'd have me, which was about every eight weeks or so. It was actually a bar, though they had a comedy night on Tuesdays. And even though he had become a mega-star, Dane Cook would appear there whenever he was in town, mostly to try out new material and keep up his chops as a stand-up artist. Meanwhile, anyone who was anyone in the LA comedy circuit would come—Ken Jeong, Zach Galifianakis and many others. They weren't yet as well known as they would become, but they were about to break out. They were also very funny.

My point is that I was on a lot of bills with Cook, not just at Dublin's but in theatre shows where I was just one of the mid-level comics who opened for him. But we never really spoke. When Dane was around, he was all business. As I mentioned, however, I did take notice of his business acumen: at the back of any venue in which he appeared, he *always* sold merchandise. There were Dane Cook hoodies, Dane Cook ball caps, Dane Cook T-shirts, Dane Cook lighters, Dane Cook coffee mugs—the list went on and on. People lined up to buy it all. And so, a question started forming in my head.

Should I be selling merchandise, too?

When I settled back in Canada, I started small, selling Gerry Dee T-shirts, baseball hats and DVDs after my gigs. Though I didn't move a lot of stuff, I was still making a few hundred dollars more per show, and with each sale I was helping, in some small way, to get the Gerry Dee brand into the world at large. I was also learning about the art of merchandising, most often through my mistakes. For example, I had some golf shirts made with a Gerry Dee logo on them. There were no tour dates, no slogan, no photo, just the two names, first and last, back to back. No one bought them. One night, I decided to wear one onstage to promote it. That didn't work, either. It also felt a little pathetic: here I was, Gerry Dee, wearing a shirt that said, cleverly enough, "Gerry Dee."

And yet, some of the other merchandise was starting to sell, particularly as more people started coming to my shows. I increased my supply. I got shirts in different colours, different styles, with different slogans. (One example was *GoFacoff?*, which came from a bit about my Italian neighbour and the way he pronounced, "Let's go for coffee." After doing this bit at Just for Laughs, a newspaper columnist in Quebec described it as the worst joke of the entire gala.)

Pretty soon, my four-hundred-square-foot studio apartment was filled with boxes; I now slept in a bed that was surrounded by cardboard. But I ordered more stuff and started selling via my website; I shipped anywhere, until the day came when someone from the UK placed an order, and I discovered how much it cost to ship a shirt to England. After that, I shipped to anywhere in Canada.

More orders came in. Slowly, I realized how much time I was spending with all those envelopes, labels and trips to the post office. I decided to kill the online sales and concentrate on selling at my live shows. After every performance, I'd run to the back of the room and, as the MC wrapped up the show, I'd throw some shirts and hats on a table. Then I would throw on a T-shirt and stand there, selling. At the end of the night, I'd pack up my inventory and load up my truck. Though it was a lot of work, it was a decent side hustle, and I kept it up for quite a while.

Fast-forward a few years. I was married, and I no longer lived in a studio apartment. I'd also moved on to theatres and bigger venues. With bigger crowds, the merchandise sales had grown; still, the money was never huge, and I was beginning to find that selling T-shirts and hats after a show can be exhausting. Sometimes, I'd be at the back of the theatre for another hour and a half, and while this was fine for a night or two, by the end of a twenty-city tour, it became exhausting. Eventually, I started using theatre staff to sell for me, which meant I had to give them twenty percent of the gross. This ate into the profit margin, and I sadly started to feel like it wasn't worth the effort. Not to mention how much space the stuff took up in my garage.

At this point, I could have done one of three things. The first was nothing. I could have just maintained the status quo, which would've been easy. The second was to get out of merch sales altogether, which would have been easier still. Instead, I doubled down, thinking that if I sold a lot of stuff, the smaller profit margins wouldn't matter (or, at least, wouldn't matter as much). I just needed a new angle, some sparkly new trinket that the general public couldn't resist. That's when it hit me: instead of selling stuff with "Gerry Dee" on it, I'd capitalize on the success of my television show and come up with a line of clothing that bore the name "Mr. D." I started having T-shirts and hoodies made bearing the phrase "Teach Hard." I also started making clothes with the words "Property of Xavier Academy," an insider's nod to the name of the school in the show.

I'll never forget the look on my wife's face when fourteen large boxes of T-shirts and hoodies arrived on our front door. "Gerry," she said, "where are we going to put all of this stuff?"

"Don't worry," I told her. "I've got two shows in Richmond Hill this weekend and I'll get rid of most of it then."

"Are you sure?"

"Of course I'm sure. In fact, I'm pretty sure I'll get rid of *all* of it."

This is what I calculated: There would be about 1,100 people at these shows. Meanwhile, I had made up four hundred T-shirts and hoodies, which also had to do me for a show I was playing the next night in Hamilton. I wondered if I should have ordered *more*. I cursed myself as I piled the boxes into my garage. While doing so, I found a few boxes of those old Gerry Dee golf shirts, which had failed to sell four years earlier. But that was then. Now, I had my own television show. My Gerry Dee golf shirts were collectors' items. I grinned, my supply issue solved—I'd bring them to Richmond Hill as well.

The following Saturday, around five o'clock, I started to load up my SUV. It was raining, which kind of sucked, though I was thankful that the distance from my garage to my truck was only a few steps. And yet, at the back of my mind, my pride was complaining. I had a hit TV show; I shouldn't have to be doing this. I ordered myself to get over it. Four hundred items, sold over two shows, would generate a nice chunk of change. An entertainer, like an athlete, never knows how long their earning potential will last. I would be stupid not to do this, and if it meant getting a little wet in the process, so be it.

I put the last box in my truck. Every square inch was taken. One more box, and I would've had to leave it at home. I closed the trunk and headed off. After a few minutes, I reached Yonge Street and York Mills Road, a busy intersection in the north end of Toronto. I had to make a left. As I turned, I heard a thump. My heart stopped. I pulled over and looked back: about half of the boxes were in the intersection. Some had broken open, some had already been hit by other cars, all of them were getting soaked. Instantly,

I knew what had happened: the back of the truck was so tightly packed that the hatch had failed to close properly. As I was driving along, it must have popped open. That thump I'd heard? It was the first box falling out. The rest, I saw, had followed along, like schoolkids holding on to a rope.

I froze. My first thought was to leave them, to just drive away and forget that any of this had ever happened. There was one problem: they were lying in the middle of a busy intersection, which meant they were dangerous. They also had the Mr. D name all over them, and the last thing I wanted was to turn on the news that night to find out that T-shirts abandoned by a local comedian in a busy Toronto intersection had caused a pileup.

Meanwhile, cars were honking and drivers were yelling at me through opened windows. They were also navigating the slalom course my fallen boxes had formed. So I got out of the truck. I had to dodge traffic as I picked up the boxes, which I couldn't really do, as I learned that day that cardboard, once soggy, stops being cardboard at all. Every time I tried to lift one, it would fall apart, hoodies and tees scattering across the rain-saturated asphalt. Other boxes were getting nudged by cars, at which point they'd fall apart as well, scattering even more oil- and dirt-soaked merchandise across the intersection.

Still, this cleanup had to be done. I pulled the hoodie I was wearing over my head, in the hope that no one would recognize me. Then I got to it, picking up three or four shirts at a time and running them back to my truck before returning to grab a few more. Throughout, people were yelling at me and telling me to get the hell out of the intersection. All of this I could handle, so long as I got all of my ruined and waterlogged stuff back into the truck, which would then allow me to get to my gig on time.

That's when it happened. A young guy with a cruel grin rolled down his window and, I shit you not, yelled, "Hey! Gerry Dee! Got any T-shirts for sale?"

I was standing in the middle of the intersection, soaking wet, surrounded by merchandise. Stupidly, I waved. He laughed, honked his horn and drove off.

I noticed an abandoned shopping cart a short distance from the intersection. Like a desperate homeless person, I started using it to collect my destroyed goods, the drivers still honking while they manoeuvred around me. At least this worked, and I managed to salvage a few of the boxes.

I then sat in the truck, soaked with rain and sweat. Some of the T-shirts had tire tracks on them. Others had miraculously survived.

I told the story from the stage that night, thinking that, at the very least, I might get a bit out of it. I also thought, perhaps naively, that it might help sales. It didn't. I drove home with the boxes that had survived. As I did, I vowed that I was through with merchandise—I got home and loaded the still-damp boxes back into the garage, where, just as my wife had feared, they remain to this day.

As for Dane Cook, he's still a well-known comic, although he doesn't have his rock-star status anymore. Regardless of what you think about his act, I saw him destroy that weekend in Tempe over twenty years ago, and it was the first time I had seen a comedian, in person, do it to that extent. Dane did what we are all trying to do as comics. Soon after, he was selling out arenas. Very few will probably ever do that, and that includes me. He taught me a lot about grind and hustle. I have now moved on to larger venues myself. Nothing like Dane did, though. I also still have a lot of hoodies and T-shirts in my garage.

# FISHING WITH THE NIECES

It's often said that there are no guarantees in the entertainment business. This is true. And yet, there are a few ground rules that can't be broken, one of the most notable being: an agent will only take you on if they think they can make money from you. This may sound a bit harsh, particularly since you need an agent to become popular enough to make an agent money. But the fact remains: if you can't put asses in seats, or get on television, an agent will not touch you.

In 2007, I placed third on *Last Comic Standing*. While I had a Canadian agent, I didn't have an American one. I badly wanted one. The United States has ten times as many people as Canada, and as a result, you can make ten times as much money there. Actually, it's probably more. The United States is the media capital of the world, meaning that if you can make ten times the money down there, you can enjoy a *hundred* times the exposure, which you can parlay into more fame, and more success, and more respect. There's a reason why most of Canada's greatest comedic minds, from John Candy to Dan Aykroyd to Mike Myers to Jim Carrey, have worked extensively in the United States. All successful, all rich and all very famous.

After *Last Comic*, I started getting phone calls from American agents. This, I have to say, was nice. I also met a bunch of agents during the taping of the show: they seemed to be just hanging around the green room, handing out business cards and suggesting that the two of us should, perhaps, in the very near future, get together for a coffee— would that work for you, Gerry? The first one I seriously talked to was recommended to me by American comedian Lavell Crawford. While I don't remember much about our initial conversation, I do remember telling him, "You know, I really don't want to be travelling to the US for, like, thirty weekends a year."

"Thirty?" he said. "I'm going to need you down here for *fifty-two* weekends a year. In fact, it'd probably be better if you moved down here."

This was a problem. My daughter, Aly, had been born on July 28 of that year, in the middle of my run on *Last Comic Standing*. Now that the ensuing tour was finally over, the last thing I wanted to do was commit to constant travel in the US. Another key point: Lavell's agent was actually a manager, which meant that, should I sign, I'd be giving him a percentage on *top* of the percentage I'd be giving to any booking agent he happened to use. (This arrangement is quite common in the States.) I declined, then talked to a few more agents before finally meeting one who seemed comfortable with me being my own manager and spending most of my time off in Toronto with my wife and new baby.

I was thrilled. While he wasn't with William Morris or any other agency of that magnitude, he *was* from a well-respected second-tier American outfit, and I really believed he might be my stepping stone into the US market. At the same time, I was skeptical. Would another agent really make that much of a difference? I had my answer a week later, when he phoned.

"Hey, Gerry, I have a gig for you in the Bahamas."

"Yeah, right."

You see, most of my calls from my agent in Canada at that point had been along these lines: "Hey, Gerry, I have a gig for you in South Porcupine. Pays seven hundred dollars. About a six-hour drive. They will give you an extra seventy-five dollars for gas, and you get a room at the Super 8. Oh, and I need you to drive two other comics."

The Bahamas! He could have stopped right there and I would have done the gig for free. Are you kidding me? A trip to the Bahamas to perform comedy? I could have quit comedy right then and there and felt like I had made it.

But he continued. There was more to this magical gig.

"Pays ten thousand dollars."

Okay, now I *knew* he was messing with me. What a cruel joke.

"Very funny. How much does it pay?"

"Ten thousand."

Silence. Was he still messing with me?

"You there?" he asked.

"Yes. Is this a joke?"

He laughed. "No." He continued as though this was a normal amount for a gig. "They will fly you in on Thursday and back out on Friday. Do you want to fly from Toronto?"

He wasn't kidding. Holy shit! My mind was racing. This was now the best gig I had ever had.

You see, when I left teaching in 2003, I was probably bringing in about seven hundred dollars a week, net. It was a good-paying job and I enjoyed it. Nobody teaches for the money, but the salary is fair in many regards. When I started to make a few bucks doing stand-up, teaching supplemented my income very well, but it would've taken me about four months to make ten thousand dollars teaching. I had never looked at it that way until this phone call. Ten thousand dollars to perform forty-five minutes of stand-up comedy for two hundred people must have been the easiest money ever made in the world since the birth of Jesus. I almost felt bad for the people paying me. I felt like I was ripping them off. And I couldn't help but think what a deal the people in South Porcupine had been getting a few months earlier.

Then, as most Canadian entertainers do when they book something in the States, I asked, "Is that US dollars?"

It was. It *always* was. The US never thinks in any other currency. As far as I'm concerned, they don't even know we get paid in Canadian dollars.

So the magic continued. Based on the exchange rate, I added another thirty percent in my head. Now, I didn't get into stand-up comedy for the money, but this was quickly becoming about the money. It was definitely an exciting moment. My wife and I had just had our first child and bought our first house. This offer couldn't have come at a better time. I ended that call with my agent by saying, "Well, this is a great start."

"Hey," he said in that ultra-casual voice, "get used to it."

Two months later, I took a United Airlines flight to Nassau, the capital of the Bahamas. From there, I took a small, sixteen-seat plane to a tiny airport on the island of Great Abaco. From there, I took a taxi to a resort about twenty minutes away. I remember being surprised by the venue itself. Given how much they were paying me, I thought it would be a world-class resort. Instead, I saw a series of small, well-appointed villas, and nothing else. If there was a pool, I never found it. There was also no one there. I wandered around, trying to find someone, calling out, "Hello? Anybody here?" After a bit, I started to think that maybe I'd been taken to the wrong spot, which would have been a problem, given that my taxi had already driven off.

I found a building that looked like it might contain a reception desk. I went inside and found a front desk manned by a young local guy. As he signed me in, I asked if he could tell me something.

"Sure," he said.

"Where *is* everybody?"

He looked at me, eyebrows raised, as though I was stupid. "They're all out on the water. You *do* know that we're hosting a marlin fishing tournament, don't you?"

"Oh, right," I said, recalling my agent's words: "It's some kind of fishing resort." If I felt a little better, it was because it was all starting to make sense. The guests were here to fish. They were all out fishing. They would come in at the end of the day, eat dinner and laugh uproariously at my material.

I checked into a room in one of the villas. I remember feeling lonely. It was hours until nine o'clock, the start time of my gig, and the room didn't have cable. I ordered dinner from room service and ate by myself, then wandered over to the venue. As the resort didn't have a formal restaurant, meals were served in a covered outdoor pavilion. Apparently, I'd be doing the gig here. A few of the resort staff were arranging chairs in a semicircle around a small, elevated platform. I went up to one of them.

"So," I said, "what kind of customers do you get here?"

He stopped, and, like the receptionist, looked at me strangely. "To tell you the truth," he said, "it's a lot of old men and their nieces."

To which I thought, *Great. It's a family place. I'm a clean comic, more or less. It'll be perfect for my act.* Again, I felt a little better. I looked out over the water, where the guests were just starting to come in after a day of fishing. My eyes widened. These were not fishing boats. These weren't even fishing yachts. These were just plain yachts, hundreds of feet long, with on-board pools and wet bars, most of them towing smaller boats that, I guessed, the owners had used for the actual fishing.

"It's something, isn't it?" said the hotel guy.

"Jesus," I said.

"Some of those boats are worth a hundred million dollars."

"My God."

"I know," he said. "I *know*."

The fishermen were now piloting the smaller boats toward a row of jetties. As they began tying off, I noticed a few things about the people who would be my audience that night. As I'd been told, the vast majority were older men. They were also loud, doughy, red in the face and drunk. A good half of them were accompanied by young, beautiful women, at which point I noticed that these "nieces" were all wearing short skirts, revealing tops and gobs of makeup. *Strange*, I thought, *that they would doll themselves up for* . . . I stopped and swallowed.

So *this*, I thought, is what the hotel employee had meant by "nieces."

They were now striding toward the pavilion, this parade of overweight millionaires, reeking of Budweiser and suntan lotion, dressed in deck shoes, Bermuda shorts and sweat-stained polos. As they attacked a buffet that the staff had put out in the pavilion, they were yelling out to one another.

"Hey, Steve, you see the one I got?"

"Hey, Mike, better luck tomorrow, you son of a bitch you!"

I stood there, watching them, wondering what I had gotten myself into.

I remember looking over at the improvised stage where I'd be performing. There was no stool, no glass of water, no sign, just a microphone on the floor. I remember thinking it looked a little like a dead fish.

The fishermen and their nieces were now seating themselves in the chairs that the staff had put out for my performance. As they waited, they ate barbecued chicken and conch salad. Once they'd finished eating and had settled themselves, I was to go on and maybe, just maybe, have a half-decent set. Just then, some guy ran onto the stage, picked up the mic and said, "Hey, everybody, we've got a comic for you."

That was it. No introduction, no warm-up, he just handed me the mic. I introduced myself and launched into my first bit: "So, for those of you who don't know, I used to be a schoolteacher, and boy, I gotta tell ya, some kids are smarter than others . . ."

In comedy, heckling does occur. I accept that. Comics like Richard Pryor, Jimmy Carr and Bill Burr built some pretty famous material from being heckled. Yet there is a code, an accepted mode of conduct, whereby the audience waits, giving you time to start bombing before they start hurling insults. To do otherwise is to violate the Geneva Conventions of comedy.

In this case, I was five seconds into my act when some slurring old fisherman yelled, "Say something funny!"

More context: In clubs, the patrons don't know each other, so they tend not to gang up on you. Yet, as soon as drunk fisherman number one yelled, "Say something funny!" his equally hammered buddy called out, "Yeah, be funny!" which cued *his* buddy, and then *his* buddy, and my audience quickly turned into a small army of loaded, perspiring hecklers.

A final bit of context: When people heckle in audiences, the heckler's companion, normally a far less drunk husband or wife, will feel embarrassed and attempt to, if not silence the heckler, tone them down a little. Not so this time. The nieces were being paid to be good company, meaning that they mostly sat on their hands, saying nothing, looking bored.

And I tried. I really did. If I'd had a raunchy act, like Andrew Dice Clay's or the late Sam Kinison's, I might've been able to feed off their hostility. But there I was, Gerry Dee, a polite ex-teacher from Canada, telling stories about the educational system. Those in the audience who weren't heckling weren't *listening*, as they were too busy talking to their friends or bragging to their nieces. This, in some ways, was even worse.

After twenty minutes or so of drunken, loud-mouthed, moronic abuse, I decided to take them on. I'd insult them about anything I could find. Their shirt. Their hair. Their drunken state. The one thing I didn't do was make fun of their companions, since I felt sorry for them. It didn't matter. Nothing worked; they were a team now and I was just a lonely, suffering comic. The heckling was getting to me. I could *hear* myself sounding desperate instead of funny. In short order, the heckling turned into meaningless yelling, into cutlery falling onto plates, into hollering for more drinks. I remember one guy, completely ignoring my act, calling across the pavilion, "Hey, Steve, when're you hitting the water tomorrow?" It was like I wasn't even there. How I wished that were true.

I kept going. In comedy, you don't have to kill to get paid. You do, however, have to finish, and I didn't want to give the management any reason not to pay me the ten thousand American dollars. So I kept on, mumbling my way through my act, the fishermen having lost interest in me altogether. Soon, they started to get up and leave. It's called "walking a room," and while it's the most humiliating thing that can happen to a comic, I was pleased, as there's an exception to the you-have-to-finish-to-get-paid rule: if you don't have an audience, you don't have to keep going. So I watched them, one by one, waving plump hands in front of their noses as if I were making a foul smell and then walking off, their nieces obediently following along behind. Two hundred became a hundred and fifty. A hundred and fifty became a hundred. A hundred became . . . six. Six fishermen lasted through the entire show. I don't know why they stayed; perhaps all that sun and liquor had finally caught up to them and they were physically too tired to get up. Or maybe they liked my act. If that was the case, they sure didn't show it: one or two of them had nodded off.

I finished with my best bit—or, at least, what I *thought* was my best bit—about a slow reader in my Grade 6 class named Bruno. There was no laughter, no applause, no recognition that I'd stuck it through to the bitter end. Even the staff weren't listening. I put down the microphone and walked to my cabin, where I desperately tried to arrange an earlier flight back to Nassau. There wasn't one. I hid in my room until noon the next day, then slunk away.

What did I learn from that experience? Many things, actually.

1. I learned to sniff out a sketchy gig.
2. I learned that if you *do* suspect that the gig is sketchy, charge the moon.
3. I learned that if the gig is at a fishing resort full of drunken idiots, don't go on at nine. Tell them you want to go on at six. This way, the audience won't be as loaded.
4. When hit by a tsunami of hatred, a wave of hostility so towering that nothing you can possibly do would salvage your act, don't even bother. Don't engage. Just do your set, get paid and get the hell out.
5. When your agent next phones you, do *not* get all pissy about the hellish experience he's just put you through, as it might mean that he'll feel underappreciated and won't then land you the next gig, one that's well paying *and* enjoyable. Instead, when he asks you how it went, you adopt his calm, ocean-breeze vocal tone and say, "The audience was a bit tough," to which he'll say, "That happens."

A couple of weeks later, I received a cheque for about thirteen thousand Canadian dollars (minus, of course, my agent's fifteen percent). I used it to buy a crib and a stroller, which we hadn't been able to afford, given how tapped out we were following the purchase of our house.

This brings me to the final, and arguably most important, thing I learned about my trip to the Bahamas. Every day, when I took Aly out for a walk in the stroller, I was reminded that gigging in front of rich, drunk marlin fishermen might not be the easiest thing in the world, but it does have one thing going for it.

At the very least, it pays the bills.

# THEN MR. D HAPPENED

For every comic who's had success in the business, there comes a time when you have to leap from being known by other comics to just being *known*. It's called the Big Break—when Jerry Seinfeld first appeared on Carson, when Sam Kinison first did his world-hunger bit on Letterman, when Chris Farley first stomped onto the *Saturday Night Live* stage as the inspirational speaker Matt Foley. It's that tipping point, that glorious trial by fire that takes a comic from playing clubs to playing theatres, from living in a basement apartment to owning a house, from taking the subway to buying a car. For me, it happened when I appeared on a reality show called *Last Comic Standing*.

Debuting in 2003, *Last Comic Standing* melded stand-up comedy with the reality show *Survivor*. Ten comics lived together in a house, and each week the comics performed a comedy challenge. They'd have to give an impromptu performance at a laundromat, say, or slip in a set while working as a city tour guide. Whoever the judges thought were the funniest won immunity, just like in *Survivor*, meaning they were guaranteed to keep their spot in the house. At the end of the show, all of the comics, addressing the camera with a sort of guilty satisfaction, put the name of one of the house's other occupants on a card reading, "I think I'm funnier than _____." The comic whose name came up most often was out. As in *Survivor*, there was a lot of plotting, scheming and alliances, perhaps not surprising given that staying on in the house meant that another four million viewers or so would watch you the following week.

There was also prize money and some sort of performing deal for the winner. It varied from season to season. But it all paled in comparison to those four million pairs of eyeballs watching you every week. From its first episode, *Last Comic* became the holy grail for comics. Unless you were already famous, you just *had* to get on.

And so, everyone tried.

In 2004, I had just moved to Los Angeles and was not doing particularly well. I decided to try out for the second season of *Last Comic*. The producers were holding open casting calls in sixty American cities, the idea being that anybody, whether they were a working comic or not, could become America's next big thing. Comics lined up by the hundreds, which provided the producers with footage of wide-eyed hopefuls, practising their bits before they got in. It was mostly staged, since comics who aren't working are rarely any good, and those who did try out in the open sessions were rarely selected. However, any comic with a decent agent or manager could schedule an audition. This included me.

At the appointed time, I went to the Hollywood Improv and did a three-minute set. I really thought it would be easy for me to get past the first stage; how wrong I was. Every comic who had ever stepped on a stage was trying to get on the show, and this included every comic in Los Angeles who was funnier and more experienced than me. The audition came and went pretty quickly, and my dream of landing on US network television was over. Again. For now.

By the time season four auditions rolled around, I was back in Canada. I reached out to those involved in the show and they gave me an audition spot in Chicago. It turned out I had been on their radar from the first time they met me, and that helped me secure this audition. I travelled to Chicago on my own dime and booked a hotel for one night in order to get ready to perform the next day at Zanies Comedy Club. The hope was to land a place among the final forty. From there, the producers would choose a group of ten to enter the house *and* the show. It was still a long shot, and I still had a lot of great comics to beat. I would do some bits on my days teaching—at this point in my career, *most* of my bits were about teaching. I'd found that I was one of a few comics who could give a first-hand look at the inside world of teaching. So, that's what I did. And it worked.

My name was the first to be chosen from Chicago to advance to the next round. Nikki Glaser and John Roy were the other two. We would all head to LA to perform in front of a large audience—and the judges again—to see if we could make the top ten. I did well, but didn't quite make it to the final ten. I did get a bit more airtime, though, so it certainly was worth the experience. And I had gotten closer to getting on the show.

When season five rolled around, in 2007, the producers were now holding auditions in the UK, Australia and Canada as well as the United States. I went to the one in Montreal, the only one in Canada. Again, I made the top forty. I flew to LA and tried to make the top ten. By now, the producers knew me quite well, which was in my favour. With some material about my recent wedding, and some more bits about my years as a teacher, I was selected to be one of the ten contestants on the show. That year, the winner would get $250,000, a development deal with NBC and pretty much instant success in the United States.

Another bit of good luck? They had changed the format of the show and had gotten rid of the contestants' house. This meant I wouldn't have to live in California for the entire time. Instead, I'd shoot for a week in Los Angeles, then fly home to spend a week with Heather, who was about five months pregnant with our first child. I don't think this is what Heather signed up for: move to a new city, get married, have a child and then pretty much raise it alone for the first six months. But she rarely said a word and knew this was an opportunity to change our lives. So, off I went.

Usually, I'd be in Los Angeles for a week at a time, after which I'd fly home for a few days, only to fly back again.

Each week, we'd perform some silly challenge, which would eliminate one or two of us. I never won any of the challenges, which meant I was on the chopping block each week. That's where strategy started to play a role. We literally built alliances with each other, like you see on *Survivor* or *Big Brother*. It wasn't as ruthless, but it still happened. Week after week, we would face challenges and vote on who we thought we were funnier than. We literally said that in the voting booth: "I know I'm funnier than so-and-so." The two with the most votes would perform at the Alex Theatre in Los Angeles, and the live audience would send someone home. Once the final five were chosen, the home audience in the US, Canada, the UK and Australia would handle the voting. I knew that making it to the top five would be life-changing. It would mean way more airtime, as well as a sixty-city live theatre tour at the end of the season. After weeks and weeks of stress, strategy and performing, I had made the top five. That's when things really started to get serious.

The competition was fierce. Ralph Harris was a seasoned comic from Pittsburgh who already had a long list of television credits. Lavell Crawford was a brilliant comic who would later become known for playing Saul Goodman's muscle for hire on *Breaking Bad* and *Better Call Saul*. Jon Reep was a Southern comic who was already well known for the line "That thing got a Hemi?" from a series of Dodge truck commercials that had aired a few years earlier. The final contestant was none other than Amy Schumer, who was the youngest of the group. Meanwhile, my wife was coming closer and closer to her due date, which was supposed to be early August, a date that, with any luck, would coincide with my week off.

It didn't. Aly was born on July 28, 2007, when I was in Los Angeles to shoot the episode of *Last Comic* in which Ralph Harris was voted off, leaving just four of us in the running. I remember my brother-in-law calling me to tell me I had a baby girl. It was the greatest call I've ever had. I became very emotional because missing her birth had not been in the plans for either of us. It's not a day you can get back. But Heather and I both knew this show was a huge opportunity. I hung up after that call and had to refocus on the show.

A short time later, I got to go home for a couple of days, just long enough to meet Aly for the first time. While all the other comics seemed to have a bottomless fountain of jokes, I was running out of material by now, and the pressure to come up with new stuff grew more intense as each week passed. The producers also told me they didn't want to see any more teaching material. I remember holding our baby while, at the same time, trying to write a bit I would perform on international television just a few days later.

And the rules were strict. Before the taping, you had to send your typed set to the producers, who had to okay every word. You weren't allowed to improvise or add stuff at the last minute—something that could have helped me stretch my set to the allotted five minutes. You also weren't allowed to do *less* than your required time: before one taping, my set clocked in at just over four minutes. "Gerry," the producer told me, "we need another minute." It was that precise.

While this experience was tough on me, it was much tougher on Heather. She was alone, with no help, dealing with a newborn. She never really complained about it, but I realized later how hard that must have been for her. In her own way, she didn't want to burden me with any extra stress so she kept it all in. Without her, I wouldn't have gotten as far as I did, on that show or in my career in general.

Back in LA, Amy Schumer was next to be knocked out, leaving Lavell Crawford, Jon Reep and me. By this point, I couldn't wait to get home and start spending time with my wife and daughter. Yet, as I mentioned earlier, the top five would have to do that tour across the USA. I knew this was in the contract, but I was the only contestant in the top five who had a newborn child at home. Heather had been holding down the fort, yet I knew it was taking a toll on her mental health, spending sleepless night after sleepless night with very little help. (She is also not the type of person to ask for assistance.)

As much as the tour would help advance my career and our financial prospects, the money wasn't good enough to have Heather go through another seventy days of parenting alone. They were offering me a thousand dollars a city. While sixty thousand dollars would have helped us start our family, it still wasn't enough to warrant me doing it. I also didn't *want* to do it, since it meant living on a tour bus for about ten weeks, performing in a different city night after night. I tried to get out of the commitment, tried to obtain more money, tried to miss some of the dates. No such luck. I was obligated to do it all, and to be honest, I understood that.

So, we decided that Heather and Aly would fly back home to Glace Bay, Nova Scotia, where her parents could help.

There was another problem. I was getting a lot of emails from fans in the eastern part of Canada, all of whom were telling me the same thing: for some reason, when they called in to vote for me, the line wouldn't work. I spoke to the producers of the show, who told me there was some glitch and they would get to it. They didn't. As I had a lot of support in the east—I'd gone to university in Nova Scotia, and my wife was from there—I figured there was no way I could win without their votes.

It was time to perform against Lavell and Jon. I was up first. I started with my bit about how much more responsible women are compared to men when it comes to drinking and driving. The theme of the whole set was the differences between men and women when they go out. I ended with an impression of every man walking into a strip joint. "Look at that guy in the front, he's here every week. What a loser!" Nothing too outside the box, but the material worked.

After the show, the TV audience voted. The results would be revealed at another taping a day later. In the meantime, the producers decided to shoot advance footage of each of us, running jubilantly into the theatre when we realized we'd made it to the final two. They spent a ton of time with Lavell and Jon, shooting their reactions again and again until the producers were satisfied. When it came to me, they did a single take. They already knew the outcome, and I would be the next to be voted off. Jon Reep ended up winning.

I flew home, spent way too little time with my wife and daughter, and then had to go on the road with Jon, Lavell, Amy and Ralph. It was a real grind. We'd already spent twenty weeks shooting a reality show together, and now faced another long haul, travelling from gig to gig on a bus. We spent a lot of time together on that bus and really got to know each other. I wish I had some stories of fighting and drama, but I don't. We really all got along very well.

Meanwhile, I was up late every night, performing, which was a shock to my system—as a teacher, I was used to going to bed at nine thirty. We'd all go out afterward, just to unwind, and most nights I wouldn't get to sleep until dawn. We'd sleep in late, get on the bus, drive several hours to the next stop, check in, grab a bite and perform. It was exhausting. All I could do was count the days until it was over. I was missing moments with my newborn daughter that I knew I could never get back, like waking up through the night to comfort her or dealing with her first diaper change or throw-up. Okay, maybe it wasn't so bad being away.

There was, however, a huge consolation: I was now getting recognized. This was new to me. Prior to *Last Comic Standing*, I'd get spotted in public a few times a year. But now, it was happening every night. People would call out to me, "Gerry Dee?" or "Loved you on *Last Comic Standing*!" or "You had my vote, man." While it was good for my ego—I'd never signed so many autographs or posed for so many photos—it also assured me that *Last Comic* had done what it was supposed to do. Suddenly, my name was all over Facebook, Twitter and comedy chat rooms. My act was getting reviewed in major publications. Agents and managers were returning my calls. One time, during a day off in Massachusetts, I went to a New England Patriots football game. I got out of my seat to use the bathroom, and I could hear people shouting my name. It was surreal.

I returned home to Toronto. Shortly after, I received a call from Anthony Cicione, who was head of programming at The Score, a sports news outlet based in Toronto. I already knew him. Back in 2003, I'd pitched him an idea for a series of comic shorts in which I played a guy who, for no apparent reason, believed he was the world's best competitor at any given sport. While the segments never took off, they were still a significant step for me. The character was stupid, oblivious and arrogant, and as such, was really the genesis of what would eventually become Mr. D.

Fast-forward four years. I now had some heat from *Last Comic Standing*, and Cicione suggested we do something together. I pitched him another idea I had, in which I would interview major sports figures, the gag being that I'd be the most arrogant, forthright sports reporter that Canada has ever seen. He loved the idea. *I* loved the idea. As well as being funny, this new bit would mean that The Score would give me media credentials, and I could walk into any post-game dressing room I wanted and just start asking questions.

About a week later, I found myself in the Toronto Maple Leafs dressing room with a cameraman, my media affiliation displayed on a lanyard around my neck. As The Score often sent actual sports reporters into dressing rooms, no one paid me much attention—I was just another guy wanting a post-game clip. (Thankfully, it seemed that none of the Leafs had watched *Last Comic*.) I spotted Matt Stajan, a Leafs centre, and asked him if he'd like to do an on-camera interview. He said yes. I crowded in really tight—so tight that my face was about an inch away from his.

"Sorry, man," I said. "I gotta be in tight on this one. My cameraman forgot to bring the right lens."

"It's a little weird," he said.

"I know, I know, I apologize." I turned to my cameraman. "Danny," I said, "do you have a seventeen you can bring in or something for this?"

There is no such thing as a "seventeen." Still, I rolled my eyes and got in even tighter, my face all but touching Stajan's, and did my made-up interview. And that was it: the birth of "Gerry Dee, Sports Reporter."

That very same night, I saw defenceman Andy Wozniewski sitting by himself in his stall. He agreed to an interview. I faced the camera. Had Matt Stajan been watching, he would have wondered why I no longer had to stand so close to my interview subject.

"I'm here with . . ." I paused and looked up at the nameplate above his stall. "I'm here with Andy Woz-ni-ew-ski." He corrected my pronunciation.

"Are you sure?" I asked. He was sure. He wasn't enjoying this, either, but that was the point. It was for the viewer, not the athlete.

The interview proceeded. Again, I asked the blandest questions I could think of. Each time I addressed Wozniewski by name, I'd say it and look up at his nameplate, the gag being that, on top of not knowing who I was interviewing, I was too stupid to learn his name, no matter how many times I looked up at his nameplate. (Years later, I ran into Stajan. He told me that, after I'd left, he and Wozniewski spoke in the treatment room and said, "Who was that idiot from The Score?")

A week later, I ended up interviewing Kyle Chipchura of the Montreal Canadiens. After shaking his hand, I tucked my microphone under my arm, took out some hand sanitizer and wiped it on my hands. Every time I asked him a question, I'd make sure to stick the microphone really close to his mouth. Then, before putting the mic to *my* mouth, I'd make sure to wipe it against my sweater. The toughest part was to stay in character and let the athlete squirm.

I'd then go away, and my producer and now great friend, Randy Urban, would edit the interviews into quick, little five-minute spots. The Score started running these whenever they had a few minutes to fill. Immediately, they blew up. Pretty soon, they were running about a hundred times a week. It now felt like I was better known for "Gerry Dee, Sports Reporter" than I was as the guy who'd placed third on *Last Comic Standing*. At one point, I got an email from some college guys who said they'd leave The Score on all day long. Every time they heard the "Gerry Dee, Sports Reporter" theme music, they'd all run into the living room and watch. Soon after, I diversified and started interviewing anyone famous. In character, I interviewed Kevin Costner and Samuel L. Jackson at the Canadian Open at Glen Abbey

Golf Club, and Jason Alexander at a poker tournament in the Bahamas. In time, I could no longer get the drop on my Canadian interview subjects, as they all knew my character was a spoof. Rather than retiring the bit, I changed the nature of it and started asking ridiculous questions.

One of my favourites from that era was my interview with Chris Bosh of the Toronto Raptors. Chris had gone to university for one year, so I drilled him on how he thought he could be successful with only one year of college. He was great and totally played along. One year, at the NHL All-Star Game, I got a hold of Steven Stamkos, Andrew Cogliano, Kris Versteeg and Dave Bolland. I ran through some basic math and geography questions with them to prove that hockey players were brighter than people gave them credit for.

"What is the capital of Australia?" I asked.

"Sydney," they all answered.

"Correct!" I said. (It's Canberra.)

"Yes!" they exclaimed.

"Next question: What is four to the power of zero?"

"Zero," said Stamkos.

"Correct!" (It's actually one.)

"Yes!"

To this day, I don't know if they ever realized they got all the answers wrong.

By now, I was starting to get a bit better known. My appearance fees were going up, and my agent was starting to land me more auditions for TV and film roles, despite my having done little in the way of acting. At one audition,

GERRY DEE

I read for the part of Wayne Cashman, the famous Boston Bruins winger, for a CBC miniseries about the historic Canada–Russia Summit Series in 1972. Apparently, they needed actors who could skate.

One of the producers was a guy named Michael Volpe, who is perhaps best known as one of the producers of *Trailer Park Boys*. We spent most of the audition talking about the fact that I had played university hockey at St. Francis Xavier in Antigonish, Nova Scotia. It turned out he had played for St. Mary's in Halifax and had been drafted by the New York Islanders. So he appreciated that I played university hockey. Now, he had to see if I could act.

To be honest, I didn't really know if I could. By now, I had taken a few acting lessons at the suggestion of my agent, but I'd found them a waste of time. Acting, for me, was just pretending—pretend you're mad, pretend you're sad, and so on. This audition involved pretending that I was a hockey player, which I *had* been, so I didn't focus on acting like a hockey player; I just concentrated on my years of playing and spewed out my lines. It worked: I was cast as Cashman. It was the start of my acting career, and it couldn't have gone better. I spent thirty-six days in Fredericton, New Brunswick, with a bunch of actors and hockey players, filming the most iconic Canadian hockey story of all time. I was hooked.

Mike and I kept in touch. He was so supportive and always so complimentary. After he got me the role of Donny in the *Trailer Park Boys* movie, we started to discuss the idea of working on something. This led to the question that every producer or production company exec is born to ask: "Do you have any ideas?"

I did. Volpe and I, along with producer Barrie Dunn, quickly worked up a pitch for a show about the world's worst life coach. This went nowhere. In a meeting in his offices in Halifax, Mike asked if I had any other ideas.

"I do," I told him, even though I didn't. It was one of those moments in which you move your lips and just pray that your brain comes up with something.

"And it is?"

I paused. I squirmed. Then it hit me: "What about a show that, you know, has to do with my years of teaching?"

"Hmmm," he said. "You're right, that's the show."

And so, *Mr. D* was born. In our minds, it would be a show that snatched the witless, arrogant, moronic character I played in The Score interviews and reinvent him, once more, as a teacher. We'd draw upon some of the real-life stories of my teaching career and build a show around that. We came up with a pitch document, sent it to the CBC, and they passed. We pitched it to CTV. They passed. By then, I was starting to realize how hard it would be to get a show. Networks in Canada get hundreds and hundreds of comedy show pitches each year, and usually, only about three or four are lucky enough to get green-lit. As much as we thought we had a great idea, we still had to find a way to make it stand out on the page, as well as stand out from the other hundreds of pitches the networks received.

This was the summer of 2008. I was booked to perform at Just for Laughs in Montreal. Before it opened, the festival asked me to take part in a press conference in Toronto. I was surprised, since only the very top acts did the press conferences, but I was coming off my successful run on *Last Comic Standing*, and "Gerry Dee, Sports Reporter" was getting bigger, so I'm sure that had something to do with it. The CBC was there. So was CTV. After the press conference, a couple of CTV executives pulled me aside and asked if they could meet with me again to discuss looking at *Mr. D* a second time. Mike and I had a call with them, and we re-pitched the show, with some changes. They passed a second time. Mike and I decided to take the show back to the CBC for a second time—the personnel had changed by now, and the landscape of comedy shows is always changing, so it was worth a shot.

This time, they commissioned a script for a pilot. That was a big first step. There was one catch, however: they wanted someone other than me to write it. Knowing that I didn't have a lot of bargaining power—they'd said no once, and it wasn't hard to imagine them saying no again—I agreed. I had also never written a script before, so it made complete sense. They suggested a writer who had some experience in writing comedy. While that script didn't work, the CBC still believed in the concept, so they suggested another writer. This one worked hard to balance the notes he was getting from us with the notes he was getting from CBC. He turned in a decent pilot script, but it still never felt like the show Mike and I had envisioned. However, the CBC agreed to shoot the pilot—another big step forward—which they tested with a sample audience. It did not test well. They passed on the show.

I was devastated. I felt like I should have spoken up more about some of their suggestions for that pilot, but we both knew we had to try to manage their expectations with our own creative vision—it's always a juggling act for everyone involved. And now, it was over that quickly. All our hopes of having a sitcom had ended. After multiple pitches, multiple scripts and a pilot, the CBC had turned down the show.

Thinking I had nothing to lose, I phoned the head of English-language services at the CBC. I hardly knew her, and I don't know what I was hoping to get out of the call, but I really wanted to tell her how much I thought this show would work.

While I can't remember what I actually said to her, I remember pointing out that I needed to be more involved in the writing process. The show needed a teacher's voice to provide the sort of authenticity that would make the show work. On and on I went, like a carnival barker pitching a sideshow act, until finally she said, "Gerry, okay, we'll commission another script."

By this time, the heads of comedy at CBC had changed again. While they agreed that the show needed my voice, they felt I needed to hire an actual writer to help me. Mike and I conducted some interviews and hired a pair of brothers to co-write the second pilot with me. Then Mike and I made a lot of changes to that script and we submitted it.

Meanwhile, my wife and I had just purchased a house that was way more expensive than we could afford. It was the old story: our agent had found a house he thought we might like, and even though it was way beyond our budget, he wanted to show it to us, just so that we could *see* what was out there. We loved it. I wanted to buy it. Heather pointed out that we couldn't afford it. I told her not to worry. "I don't know *how*," I told her, "but it'll work out. It just will, Heather."

So we bought it. On the day we moved in—a day that should have been a joyful start of our new lives in a new house—I was literally sitting in the passenger seat of the moving truck when my phone rang. It was the CBC. They had passed on the show again. They weren't even going to shoot a pilot this time. I was stunned. Surely, the show was now dead.

I told Heather. She was very worried. I'd banked on getting the show in order to pay for the house. "What," she pleaded, "are we going to do now?"

To this day, I'm not sure why I wasn't panicking as well. Perhaps she was upset enough for the both of us. "Don't worry," I said. "I'll figure it out."

As the movers carried furniture into a house we could no longer afford, I called the CBC and basically pleaded with them to reconsider. They said they were all fans of the show, but basically it just wasn't strong enough to pursue as a series. There was nothing more they could do.

Mike and I decided we would ask CBC for the rights to the first pilot, the one that had been filmed, to take it to other networks to see if we could sell it. We wanted permission to re-edit it and do whatever we could to pitch it elsewhere. It was not very likely that any other network would want a show that a competitor had just passed on, but it was all we had left to try.

I was at the mall with my wife and daughter when my phone rang. It was Mike. I assumed he just wanted to chat about our next steps. It turned out to be a call that changed my life.

"Hey, Gerry," he said, "I have CBC on the line. They aren't going to give us the rights to the pilot to shop around."

"What?!" I asked. "Why? What's the reason? That makes no sense if they aren't going to do anything with it!"

"I'm not sure," Mike continued. "Let me patch you into the call."

Sally from the CBC started: "Okay, guys. We aren't going to give you the rights to the pilot . . ." I was just about to jump in when she continued: "Because we're going to shoot another pilot!"

She basically sang those words. I was so confused. And excited. *Really* excited. So was Mike. The call went from being the worst in my career to the best, all in a matter of seconds.

We shot the second pilot that summer in Halifax. A few months later, the CBC called us into their offices. Mike and I had a feeling it was good news, because we *knew* they didn't call people in to give them bad news. We were right. The CBC was picking up *Mr. D*.

I called Heather to tell her we had done it. In this case, the "we" included Mike, me, and both our wives, Heather and Linda. Their support for each of us through what turned out to be a four-year process was so important.

Thirteen episodes were ordered that first year. The series premiered in January 2012 and the overnight ratings said it had been seen by 1.3 million viewers—the most for a new CBC show premiere in years.

The CBC is renowned for giving shows—especially comedies—a really good chance to find their audience. You rarely see shows cancelled after one season at the CBC. Ratings are a huge factor in a show's longevity, and during season two, ours started to slip and we were at risk of not being renewed for season three. What a lot of people don't realize is that any network has a limited amount of airtime for their shows, especially in prime time. There was a chance to put us into a different time slot for eight weeks, and Mike and I jumped at it, because a week earlier we felt we were about to be cancelled. In season four, ratings still weren't where they needed to be, and funding wasn't as readily available. In a unique twist, the CBC teamed up with Rogers Media to jointly air the season. Having both networks share in the costs allowed us to keep the show going for the fourth season, and seasons five through eight aired solely on the CBC. The show's popularity continued to grow, and we had smooth sailing through our last season.

I knew going into that eighth season that I wanted to end the show. I was lucky to get the chance to make that choice—you rarely get the chance to end a show on your own terms. But it felt like the right time to wrap things up, so I did. I will never know if we would have gotten a ninth season, and I don't want to know. In the end, there were eighty-eight episodes in all. I still miss it.

# WHEN MR. D WENT GLOBAL (ALMOST)

I n 1983, a TV show called *Star Search* premiered, in which entertainers competed in categories that included singing, dancing and comedy. In each episode, you'd compete against another performer from the same category, your performance rated by both the home audience and a panel of celebrity judges. The winners in each category would then come back and perform against other winners in the same category. Once you'd done this a few times—it varied from season to season—you'd then come back and compete against the winners of the other categories. The winner of that episode would then get a hundred thousand dollars. The show was hosted by Ed McMahon and gave us such stars as Luther Vandross, Sam Harris and the teenage sensation known professionally as Tiffany.

Though the show went off the air in 1995, it was rebooted by CBS in 2003, in large part due to the success of *American Idol*. This time, the host was Arsenio Hall. The guest judges included country singer Naomi Judd; Ben Stein, the guy who played the droning economics teacher in *Ferris Bueller's Day Off*; and Frank Zappa's son Ahmet Zappa.

One day, I was at home, watching TV, and the all-new *Star Search* came on. My first reaction was surprise, since I'd thought it had ended years before. My second reaction was *I wonder how I'd get myself on that show*.

I made a few calls. Soon, I discovered I had a small—and by small, I mean paper-thin—connection to the producers.

At the time, I was arranging to appear at an HBO Comedy Festival in Aspen, Colorado. As it turned out, the producer, a guy named Mike Wardlow, worked for one of the executive producers of *Star Search*. So Mike passed along the demo tape I'd used to get myself booked at the Aspen festival, and voila, I got a call saying I was on.

I was beyond excited. *Star Search* was American, it was on a major network, it appeared in prime time, it was viewed by millions of people. I knew that if I went on that show, it might give me a major boost. At the time, I was still working as a high school teacher. And while I won't say that I was losing my focus as a teacher, I was really beginning to feel as though it might be time to leave the classroom for good. In other words, I was at an uncomfortable spot: not quite doing well enough to leave, but doing too well to stay. This show, I figured, could change things. So I went to Los Angeles. To appear, the producers gave you $140, along with accommodations and a plane ticket. I remember that, the morning I went to the airport, I promised myself I was not going there to simply appear on a television show. I, Gerry Dee, was going to California to win it all and return home triumphant. I remember sitting in the airport, waiting in the lounge, listening to Eminem's "Lose Yourself" on my earphones, motivating myself with the lyrics. I don't think he was talking about being on *Star Search*, but to me he was.

I got to my hotel. They put me in a Holiday Inn in the middle of Hollywood. On the elevator, I met two people who were in town to appear on an episode of *Judge Judy*. I had no idea who they were or what they were doing on *Judge Judy*, but I remember thinking, *They are more famous than me*.

It was my first time in Hollywood, and this is what I honestly thought: once I won *Star Search*, I'd live here. I'd have no choice. My career would demand it of me. It was February, and the weather in Los Angeles was beautiful. *You*, I told myself, *could get used to this. You*, I told myself, *will hang out with Judge Judy one day*.

I did not sleep well that night. When I got to the studio the next morning, I met with Judi, one of the producers, who promptly told me something that I wished someone had thought to tell me a bit earlier. My set on the show would be all of ninety seconds long. Ninety seconds! I, on the other hand, was a long-form comic, a teller of stories. Even the basic set-ups of my bits took several minutes.

Meanwhile, I was supposed to preview what I was going to do on the show right then and there, so that Judi could make sure that the material worked, came in on time and, perhaps most importantly, was clean enough for network television.

The comic who was going to be my competitor was there. He was a really nice guy named Horace H.B. Sanders. When Judi announced that our set time was a minute and a half, he seemed completely unbothered. "Oh, that's no problem," I remember him saying. "I've got five or six bits that are short enough."

One of the producers then advised me on which bit she thought was my best. "You know, there was this one bit on your tape . . . the one about playing dodgeball. That one is fairly short. Why don't you do that one?"

I did the bit, in which a teacher gets revenge against a rotten kid by playing opposite them on a dodgeball court. It clocked in at three minutes.

"Hmm," she said.

"What do I do?"

"*I* know," she said. "Why don't you cap it when you say, 'You can't hit kids as a teacher, but nothing says you can't play dodgeball with them'?"

"But that's not the joke. That's the set-up to the joke."

"It doesn't matter! It's hilarious."

I knew it wasn't. It needed the ending and I was cutting off the story midway. I was about to refuse, when I remembered something important: I was a schoolteacher from Scarborough, Ontario. I drove a used car and lived in a one-room basement apartment. She, on the other hand, was a heavyweight producer who had the power to make me famous, wealthy and beloved the world over. She was also a well-known manager who often took on the entertainers who appeared on her show.

"All right," I mumbled.

"Good! It's all settled! This'll be great. I'm so excited!"

An assistant took me to the lot, where I was given a small trailer. Next to me were a pair of eleven-year-olds who were appearing in the junior dance category. On my right was a twelve-year-old who was in the junior singer category. Sanders was on the other side of the junior dancers. While I always felt a little nervous before a gig, it was a lot worse this time, since I knew I had to go out and deliver material that not only wasn't very good, but that made no sense as a story. So I sat, rocking like a madman, on the step of my trailer, Eminem blasting into my ears. Thank God I hadn't eaten.

Someone came to get Horace and me. There was a studio audience. Arsenio Hall introduced Horace. Horace went out and killed. He offered up quick jokes that landed every time. It felt like he did twenty minutes in ninety seconds. There was, I remember, a lot of applause.

"And for our next comic . . . ," Arsenio started.

I walked on. I tried to look confident as I delivered the first ninety seconds of a much longer story. Halfway through my bit, I noticed that Naomi Judd wasn't even paying attention. Instead, she was bouncing one of the junior dancers on her knee.

Finally, I came to our agreed-upon final line: "And while you can't hit a kid, you *can* play dodgeball with him."

The laughter was lukewarm. My ninety seconds felt like twenty minutes. During the judging, I got a string of sevens. Naomi Judd, I remember, said I was likeable. I wondered how she knew, given she'd been busy playing patty cake with one of the child performers. Horace, predictably, got nines and tens. Arsenio announced the winner. Horace pumped his fist into the air. The audience clapped.

I walked slowly out of the studio and tried to get a cab back to the airport. It was a warm day and I didn't have sunglasses. As I stood there, waving my arm in the air, I promised myself that I would never get that far ahead of myself. Never again, I pledged, would I ever get that excited about something that had not yet happened, no matter how much it might seem like it was, indeed, going to happen.

This, it turned out, was hard for me.

By 2015, *Mr. D* had been on air for five full seasons and was continuing to pull good numbers. I had a friend named Scott Bear who owned a few car dealerships. Scott's other claim to fame was that he'd gone to high school with none other than fellow Canadian Will Arnett, the star of *Arrested Development* and *Bojack Horseman*. At the time, Arnett was also making waves with a production company called Electric Avenue.

Whenever I saw Scott, he'd always say the same thing: "I should put you in touch with Will. You two would get along. You really would." And nothing would happen, until the next time I saw Scott. "I tell you, Gerry, I've got to introduce you to Will. I really will, you know, one of these days."

Then, one day, it happened: I got a message from Scott saying something like "Just so you know, I emailed Will about you. Hopefully, he'll get back to you."

Two hours later, I received another email. It was from Will Arnett. He said he had seen some clips of the show while watching the Leafs on *Hockey Night in Canada* and would love to chat about it. He seemed to like it.

I responded as though I received emails from people like Will Arnett every day. "Oh, hey, man, thanks for the kind words. I'm a fan of yours as well. I'd love to chat. Gerry."

Looking back on that email, I have to say that my casual tone was also a bit of a defence mechanism. I knew enough about Hollywood to know that people say things all the time, and that most of the time they don't mean them. Even though it had been exciting to get that initial email from Will, I assumed nothing would come of it.

The very next day, I got a call from Jed Weitzman, who was president of Electric Avenue and who happened to be the stepson of Henry Winkler, who played Fonzie on *Happy Days*. He was going to set up a conference call with Will, Will's manager, Will's agent and me. Peter Principato was Will's manager. Some of his other clients included Ed Helms from *The Office* and Sean Hayes from *Will & Grace*, to name a couple. Richard Weitz was Will's agent, and one of the biggest in the business. He also managed Ricky Gervais and Tina Fey. Apparently, Peter and Richard both wanted to speak to me. I couldn't believe how quickly this was happening, or that it was even happening at all. But there I was, a few days later, on the phone with some of the most powerful people in Hollywood. I believe I was standing in my kitchen. I remember trying to sound as cool as I could. You know, like it was no big deal.

It was Principato who told me their plan. "What we want to do, Gerry, is create a version of *Mr. D* for an American audience. Really, we're all such fans of the show. We think it could be a really good fit for all of us. The hope is that you would act and write in the US version." That week, I started hearing from lawyers. I hired one of my own. For the next two months, while the lawyers hammered out a contract, I spoke with Will, or Peter, or Richard, or Jed, or some combination of them, every week. Will was funny, smart and easygoing. We talked about our mutual love of the Toronto Maple Leafs and Canada in general.

Finally, there was a completed contract, in which Will Arnett and his company would purchase the rights to produce an American version of *Mr. D* from Mike Volpe and me. They signed. We signed. We could now move into actively pitching the show to US networks and streamers. Could this show be the next *The Office*? After all, this is what had happened with Ricky Gervais. But I was getting ahead of myself. *Way* ahead of myself.

I started to think of the success it would bring. The money, the fame, the house in Los Angeles. And I started commuting to LA. There always seemed to be some meeting I had to attend or some new person I needed to meet. I even began looking at houses in case we had to move there. That dream of living in Hollywood that had started with my appearance on *Star Search*? It was no longer a pipe dream. Now, it seemed like a reality.

Every year, Will Arnett hosted a gala benefit for one of the hospitals in Toronto. Shortly before the event that year, he called me up and said, "Hey, Gerry, I'd love you to come this year. I'm bringing Jed and Mitch up as well so you can all meet. You can sit with them. And bring your wife. Can you make it?"

Mitch, by the way, was Mitchell Hurwitz, the creator of *Arrested Development*.

"Of course I can make it," I said.

So I went. Heather came, too. Plates were a thousand dollars a pop—someone, presumably Will, paid for mine. Most of the guests were doctors and their partners. Will was the MC, and Chris Rock was the comedian they hired.

It was starting to feel more and more like this was all going to happen. Mitch and I would meet in LA to discuss the US version of the show. According to our plan, he and I would be co-showrunners. As such, his involvement was huge. He was a big name. He also had a first-look deal with Netflix, so having him on board meant we would get the chance to make a serious pitch to them. In addition to our meetings in LA, we'd talk via phone and email to properly set up the pitch. I learned a lot from him. The pitch process was very detailed, and we went over it several times.

I had pitched other shows and tried to get calls with people, and I can tell you: when you have Will Arnett in your corner, everything happens much more easily. When you add Mitch Hurwitz, and both of their managers and agents into the mix, people take you *very* seriously.

Our plan was to pitch first to Netflix. Instead of asking for a pilot, as the other networks all did, Netflix executives were typically known to order a full season right off the bat. Furthermore, everybody seemed to think the American

*Mr. D* would be a perfect fit for Netflix. Netflix loved Will; Netflix loved Mitch. I couldn't see how this wasn't going to happen. A meeting was set up with their head of comedy, as well as Ted Sarandos, their top content executive. Once again, my mind started to get ahead of myself. I looked at more houses and cars. And maybe a golf club.

We met at the Netflix offices on Sunset Boulevard—me, Will, Jed and Mitch with Ted and his team. Will and Jed started the introductions, and then passed it over to Mitch and me for the pitch. It went great. Sarandos seemed to enjoy it. We all left with smiles on our faces. The next few weeks would be stressful as I waited for Netflix's decision, but I have to be honest: I assumed this was a done deal, particularly with Will and Mitch involved. At least I had a few weeks to dream.

Nope.

One hour later, they had passed. They don't waste time in LA. It seemed that, because the Canadian version of the show had already been on Netflix in Canada, they didn't feel the need or desire to add a new American version.

We were all disappointed. With Mitch now out of the picture—he worked exclusively with Netflix—we had to look at attaching a new showrunner so we could take the idea to networks like CBS, Fox, NBC and ABC where I wasn't known. The networks certainly wouldn't be interested in having *me* as a showrunner, and I would later find out that I wouldn't even be *acting* in the show. I was fine with all that. The sale of the show would keep Mike and me on as producers, and it would still be a nice credit and payday on top of the pride of knowing that we had created something that would land on US television.

We prepared for another round of meetings, without Mitch *or* Will, who by this time was getting busy with *Bojack Horseman*. I was starting to sense that our chances were getting slimmer. The meetings always felt good, and I left each one feeling like the news would be good, only to hear very quickly that they had passed. After Fox, NBC, ABC and Disney turned us down, I stopped looking at houses in Los Angeles.

Our last pitch was with CBS—the same network that, ironically, had aired the *Star Search* revival—and they said yes. *Yes!* Oh. My. God. We had just sold our show to a US network. At CBS. New lawyers were brought in, and new contracts were signed. I started looking for houses once again. (Did I want a circular driveway? A home theatre? An indoor sauna? Did I *just*.)

Will and I would still exchange friendly texts and emails, but I was now mostly talking with Jed, who ran Will's company. The first text I got from Will reminded me of how proud he also was to be Canadian. It also reminded me of how quick his wit was:

"Hey, Gerry, it's 'Will A' here."

I jokingly responded, "Hey, Will A, what does the 'A' stand for so I can add you to my contacts?"

His response: "Eh."

Very quick and very Canadian.

We found a new showrunner: Tom Hertz, who'd written for shows like *Spin City* and *Rules of Engagement*. Tom was super nice and he was known at CBS, which was a must. As such, his script would automatically be looked on more favourably than anything I, a nobody from Canada, could write. I spoke to Tom a little about the characters and the show—after all, it was based on my own life. It was a bit frustrating that I would have no say in writing my own show, but I knew enough to keep my mouth shut. I was still so excited and stressed. By this point, it had been eighteen months of getting ahead of myself. Eighteen months of wonder and excitement. This, I felt, was no time to rock the boat.

I signed a contract. Jed sent me the press release that CBS was planning to put out the next day. It was pretty cool to read: "CBS acquires the rights for Canadian sitcom *Mr. D*, starring Gerry Dee," or something like that. All I remember was that my name was there. It had finally happened. Mike and I had made a few dollars, but nothing like the money we would make if CBS picked up the show. Even though I wasn't going to be acting or writing in it, the deal would help me break into the US market.

"I am *so* excited," I told Jed.

"You should be."

"Can I tell people about this?"

"Of course you can."

I hung up. As it happened, I was scheduled to do an interview later that morning with a reporter from the *Toronto Sun*. Mostly, we talked about an upcoming tour I was doing in Canada. It was fairly short, as interviews go, and at the end he asked me a stock question: "Before we wrap up, Gerry, is there anything else you're working on?"

So I told him. "Actually . . ." I told him CBS was going to produce an American version of *Mr. D*, with an American setting and American actors, not unlike what NBC had done with the American version of *The Office*. We hung up. An hour later, the reporter put his story online. It seemed to take only minutes before Jed called me, enraged.

"Gerry!" he said. "You told a *reporter*?"

"But you told me I could tell people!"

"*Friends*, you could tell. *Family*, you could tell. But a reporter? What were you *thinking*?"

"Am I in trouble?"

"It's okay. I'll smooth it over, but it's not good, Gerry. CBS is really upset."

"Jed, I'm sorry."

"Don't worry about it. Just don't tell anyone else, okay?"

I hung up. I remember turning to my wife. "You're not going to believe this," I told her, "but I think I might have just messed this all up." It was at that moment that I learned what the term "scoop the press" meant. I had just done it, and it wasn't cool.

An hour later, CBS put out its press release about the American *Mr. D* project:

> Rules of Engagement *creator Tom Hertz is back at CBS with another multi-camera comedy. The untitled project hails from Will Arnett's Electric Avenue and CBS TV Studios, where the company had a first-look deal. [The company has since moved to Sony TV, but this project stemmed from that previous tie-up.] Written by*

*Hertz, it is a workplace ensemble comedy set at a public high school. Hertz and Arnett executive produce, alongside Peter Principato of Principato-Young Entertainment, Gerry Dee and Mike Volpe. Electric Avenue's Jed Weitzman is producing.*

In other words, it had completely changed.

Shortly after that, Tom Hertz submitted his first draft of the script to the network brass. I didn't get a chance to weigh in. In fact, I didn't even get a chance to *read* it before they sent it out. It didn't matter. They turned it down. The US version of the show was done. And with that news, everyone moved on from Gerry Dee.

I learned something about myself through that process: don't get too far ahead of yourself. I'm sure I drove everybody nuts throughout it all. When you want something so bad, it doesn't always make sense to show it. I certainly showed it, and it didn't make things any easier.

As for Scott Bear, the guy who first put me in touch with Will Arnett, we're still good friends. I still buy my cars from him and I'm still forever grateful for the connection. Will is still a huge star in Hollywood. He has a full-time publicist, manager, agent, stylist and production company.

I still answer my own emails.

# LIFE AFTER MR. D

After *Mr. D* ended in 2018, I fell into a funk. I experienced what a lot of creative people go through when a lengthy project draws to an end. You can't help but think, *Okay . . . is that it?* In my case, I had nothing to fall back on but my stand-up. I knew I could go out and do a tour—and, because of *Mr. D*, sell a bunch of tickets. I also knew that, if I did another tour after that, I would sell fewer tickets. Not a lot fewer—just not as many as the tour that came before. And if I did another tour after *that*, I'd sell fewer tickets still. This was my new reality. Unless I got another project that put me before the public, this is what I had to look forward to: stand-up gigs with ever-dwindling audiences, until the day came when even the club circuit wouldn't have me, and I found myself doing unpaid open-mic gigs at one of the coffee shops on Bloor Street.

It's called catastrophic thinking. It's the way the brain works when you're stuck at home, and you have no work, and the kids are at school, and there's nothing to distract you but your own self-punishing imagination. Here were the facts, as far as I could see them: I was fifty years old. In the entertainment industry, this is ancient. My show had ended. My phone wasn't ringing. I didn't feel funny. *What*, I kept thinking, *is going to happen to me?* But then, little by little, the wheels in my head started to turn again. I started thinking of ideas for new television shows. Soon, I started feeling hopeful. This is a key characteristic of mine: when I fall, I fall hard, but for a short time only. Then, I pop up swinging.

I started pitching ideas. The CBC gave me some money to develop a show called *My Scottish Family*. (Usually, development money in Canada is somewhere between ten and twenty thousand dollars.) I wrote a script that was based on my own family's immigrant experience. I showed it to the CBC; they passed. I showed it to a bunch of other networks; they all passed as well. I remember one executive telling me that viewers would have trouble understanding the accents. Okay, then.

So I moved on. I got development money for a show called *The Golf Shop*, which took place in a high-end golf and country club. Again, I put a writers room together and we wrote some scripts. The CBC passed. The other networks passed. I moved on. I wrote a drama called *Junior* that took place in the world of junior hockey. Everyone passed. I moved on. I pitched an idea for a series based on my experience coaching minor hockey. I got development money. I wrote a script. No one bit. Then I pitched an idea for a short film called *Bar Fight*, which I adapted from a news story in the US. This went nowhere. I got seed money for a show called *Stand Up*, which would have been based on my life as a stand-up comedian. Everyone and their uncle said no. I came up with an idea called *Prison Guards*, which I wrote on my own, with no development money. Everyone passed, including all of the US networks I pitched it to. Pass, pass, pass, pass. It was a common theme. There was another show called *The Sports Reporter*, which involved my very successful character from The Score, "Gerry Dee, Sports Reporter." I pitched it to CTV. They loved it and gave me money to develop it. Then they passed.

The closest I ever got to producing an actual show during this period was an idea called *Kids That Are Kind of Amazing at Stuff*. In it, I interviewed outrageously talented children, the laughs coming from the unexpected things the interview subjects might say. Using a second round of funding, we shot a couple of episodes. I interviewed a ten-year-old concert pianist, a six-year-old geographer, an eight-year-old opera singer, a seven-year-old golfer, a thirteen-year-old opera singer. We showed the footage to CBC executives. They passed. I didn't feel bitter. The CBC was always good about giving me an opportunity to show them something new. I just hadn't nailed it yet. *Mr. D*, we nailed. The rest of the pitches, not so much.

One of my strategies for career longevity is that I don't burn bridges. I can't tell you how many times I've heard of people who've screamed or slammed doors on their way out of pitch meetings. Or who have taken to social media to bash one of the networks. It never made sense to me, and I always looked at a show being passed on as a prompt to make the next one better. It has also helped me to remember that very little content is created in Canada, while at the same time, everyone wants a television show. In any given year, network executives in Canada will take between two hundred and three hundred pitch meetings. In the USA, I imagine it's ten times that. These, by the way, are serious meetings, involving known talent, agents and credited producers. Meanwhile, at any given time, a Canadian network might have two or three sitcoms on the air.

You also have to understand the level of competition that's out there. Let's say you're an actor with an idea for a sitcom. You go to see one of the networks. One of their shows is ending, so they are considering ideas for a new show. You leave your pitch meeting feeling that things went well, that they were really interested, and that you really have a chance at getting your show off the ground. But then, the next day, the network takes a meeting with some major Hollywood stars who have a can't-miss idea. Who, I ask, do you think they are going to pick?

So I never got bitter or upset or angry—a little frustrated and discouraged, perhaps, but never angry or bitter.

I was also starting to look at acting in another sitcom, hopefully something in the US. Despite promising myself that I had given up on America following my disastrous stint living in Los Angeles, I called my agent.

"I'd love to try and get on a US show," I said.

It was something he'd been working on, but I told him to widen the net. So, he did just that. He started to send me out for US stuff. Big stuff.

"I've got an audition lined up for you," he told me one day. "It's for *Fargo*, the series."

"Awesome! When?"

"They need it by Wednesday. It's a nice role."

*Fargo* is a drama. I didn't care. I wanted to try drama and felt it was something I could do. He emailed me the sides—a few scenes from the script that I would learn for the audition. Then I dropped everything. I cancelled a doctor's appointment, a volleyball game and a lunch I had scheduled for the next day. I learned my lines. Aly, I remember, helped me. Then I figured how I was going to deliver them. I had to decide exactly who this character, a police officer, was. It's the sort of thing that can take several discussions with a director on a set. But in an audition, you only have yourself—or, in my case, a daughter who was only twelve and not particularly helpful because she couldn't even pronounce half the words in the script. And so, you pose yourself a million questions. Did this cop grow up rich or poor? Did he have a good childhood? Who does he love most in life? What kind of neighbourhood did he grow up in? What kind of music does he like? What does he want? In the case of *Fargo*, I had an extra task. I had to learn to do a Minnesota accident. I remember staying up that night, listening to the original *Fargo* movie and combing the internet for news reports coming out of Minneapolis.

The next day, I hired an audition company. There are a bunch of them in Toronto. The one I usually used was called Central Casting. For about seventy dollars, they provided me with a studio, cameras, lighting, a professional reader and a link to my audition that I could send to my agent. I went down and filmed the audition, then sent a digital copy to my agent, who, by 5 p.m., had forwarded it to the casting directors or the producers. A week or two later, my agent called them. That's right: in show business, if you don't get something, they don't call you to tell you. You just figure out that you didn't get it because nobody got back to you.

This process repeated itself. I auditioned for *Vice Principals*, the HBO series. I auditioned for the comedy *Man Seeking Woman*. Soon, I started to look for different ways of doing them. I downloaded an app that allowed you to film "professional-looking auditions" on your computer. This was a vast, vast overstatement. I bought a good camera and lights and tried filming my auditions in my basement, with Aly acting as my reader. This didn't work, either. I remember filming an audition for a hospital role, in which Aly was my scene partner. This was not a good idea. She couldn't pronounce the word *stethoscope*. So I went back to driving down to Dupont Street and paying to do my auditions.

I gave up after about thirty of these auditions. Then my agent called me about a thirty-first.

"Listen," I told him, "I'm done with these auditions. If it's for a drama, fine, but there's *so* much stuff out there of me doing comedy. Send them my reel, and if they're interested, I'm sure they will know from that." It's what bigger names did. I wasn't a bigger name, but I was confident I had done enough to showcase what I could do in a comedy. Keep in mind, too, that these were not the top roles on these shows. They were good parts, but secondary ones for sure.

"Okay, he said. "If that's what you want me to do, I'll do it."

I was back to wondering what was next for me. I had no shows in development, I had no ideas on paper, and I had just basically closed the door on US sitcoms by telling my agent I'd only take one if I was offered a part without an audition. With no other options, I had to return my attention to stand-up. I knew the crowds might be smaller, but it was all I could do. It was 2019. I had now accepted that this could be the end for now.

And then the phone rang. It was the CBC.

"Do you have a minute?" they asked.

Of course I did. After catching up for a bit, they asked, "Would you be interested in hosting *Family Feud Canada*?"

It was less than two seconds before I responded. "Yes!" I said. I had heard they were working on bringing the format to Canada, so when the opportunity came my way, I jumped at it.

I. Was. Back.

I remember the joy and relief I felt, that I could now get back to being funny on TV again. That's all I ever wanted, and I didn't want it to end. Months later, I was flown to LA to see the US version being taped. I met Steve Harvey, the host, and all he said was "Just be you." Now, Steve had no idea who I was, but I guess in his own way he was saying, "Don't try to be any of the hosts before you. Be *you*." So that's what I tried to do.

I have definitely tried to put my own spin on things—maybe it works and maybe it doesn't, but the last thing I'm going to do is try to be Steve Harvey or Ray Combs or Richard Dawson. Before I started, I researched the earlier years of the American series, which at that point was over forty years old. I remember watching the show with my parents as a kid and seeing Richard Dawson kiss every female contestant on the lips. It probably seemed so normal to do that in the '70s (and it shouldn't have been), but it was kind of creepy to watch in 2019. Ray Combs and Steve Harvey were, for me, the best hosts because they took chances and brought the comedy aspect to the show. Mostly, I watched Steve Harvey, because he brought the show to the massive level it is at right now in the US. I studied as much as I could, then tried to make it my own.

I had no idea what to expect from the show, but I can tell you this: it's much more fun than I ever could have imagined. Meeting all these great families from across Canada has been so amazing. At the end of the day, it's the families that are the real stars; I'm just there to move the game along and hopefully have some fun.

When we launched, we were looking for a moment that would get the show some attention, and it happened in the first few episodes. The question was "Name Popeye's favourite food." Eve, the contestant, said, "Chicken," and the rest is history. It was an answer based on a generation gap, but it got the show a lot of notice. When Steve Harvey retweeted the clip, I knew we were on the *Family Feud* map.

But I still missed acting. And then I got a call from my agent, Nigel.

"There's this Fox show coming up called *A Moody Christmas*." (Before it aired, the title changed to *The Moodys*.)

"Go on."

"I think you should read for it."

"I really don't want to. Send them some *Mr. D* clips or some stand-up clips or my *Trailer Park Boys* clips. If they like me, they will see from those clips."

This was a lot to ask of a producer or a network, because they write a character in a specific way and really need to see people read their lines. I knew I was sabotaging myself by saying I wouldn't audition, but as I said, I had really begun to feel that the process was a waste of time.

"Okay, he said. "I'll send your reel."

I looked up the project on IMDb, the Internet Movie Database. There were three producers. Bob Fisher had done *We're the Millers*, *Wedding Crashers* and *Married with Children*. Rob Greenberg was behind *How I Met Your Mother* and had worked on *Frasier*. Tad Quill had produced the 2015 *Odd Couple* reboot and *Spin City*. The leads in the series—which recounted the events of a highly dysfunctional family getting together over the holidays—were Denis Leary, Elizabeth Perkins and Jay Baruchel. Looking at all of this talent, I suddenly wanted to do this series very, very badly. I had to fight the impulse to call up Nigel and tell him I'd changed my mind, that I'd happily audition if it meant I had the slightest chance of actually landing the part of Denis Leary's oddball brother.

I didn't need to. Less than a week later, I got a call from Nigel.

"They loved it," Nigel said. "You got the part."

We filmed in Montreal during COVID. This presented its own set of problems. According to union rules, you could only spend fifteen minutes per day unmasked within six feet of another actor. Meanwhile, we had a COVID regulations officer who walked around with a stopwatch and a yardstick, continually on the lookout for infractions. So, let's say I had to do a three-minute scene with Denis Leary on a single shooting day. If that scene took more than fifteen minutes to shoot, the COVID officer would stop the scene and we'd have no choice but to finish the following day. This costs extra money, and networks don't like it when things cost more than they budgeted for.

It was also the middle of winter, and everyone was freezing. We took our meals alone, in cubicles. We weren't allowed to leave our rooms after eight o'clock at night because Montreal had a citywide lockdown that applied to everyone at that time. At the end of the day, there was no going out to unwind; instead, we went straight to our hotel rooms, where we spent our nights watching television. I didn't care. Denis, Elizabeth and Jay were all fantastic to work with, and beyond kind to me. All the cast were. So were the producers and directors. Bob, Rob and Tad really went out of their way to let you know how well you were doing. That means a lot to an actor. I felt like I'd won the lottery.

Here I was, on a Fox sitcom. After all those years of trying in Los Angeles, and all the agents, producers, US networks and casting directors who had said no, I had finally made it onto an American series at fifty years of age.

The show was well received. I forced myself not to let my mind get too ahead of myself. Still, I wondered: Should I be looking at living in LA again? Would a big US agency want me now? Would movies be next?

"Stop it, Gerry!" I'd have to tell myself. "Let it happen as it should."

We got renewed for a second season, and my character, Roger, was given more to do. That's a good sign in my business. Late in 2020, I was back filming in Montreal. COVID protocols had loosened a bit but were still in effect. I felt more comfortable in season two because we all knew each other better.

One day, when I got to set, I was told I had to do something I'd never done as an actor—I was going to have to cry. I remember talking to the director. "What kind of a cry is this?" I asked him. "Is it one of those cries that gets a laugh? Is that it? Am I playing it for laughs?"

"No," he said. "It's a real cry. A 'touching moment' cry."

I sat in the corner of the set, put in my earbuds and listened to my parents' favourite song, an old number called "When I Grow Too Old to Dream." It comes from the 1934 romantic musical *The Night Is Young*. It was also supposed to be the song that my parents first danced to at their wedding; the DJ made a mistake and played something else. To make amends, I played it at my wedding, so that they could dance to it then. To this day, when I think of that song, I think of my mother. It was one of the last times I remember her being able to walk and function like she used to. It was so nice to see them dance to that song. The time came. I took out my earbuds and, seconds later, did the scene. It worked.

After two episodes, the show was cancelled. Poor ratings, apparently. It happens, particularly in the US, where decisions are made and acted upon quickly. It was such a great opportunity to work on that show, and my hope was that I might now at least be on the radar of Rob, Bob and Tad, as well as the casting team at Fox.

Eighteen months later, I received the following text out of the blue: "Hey Gerry! Your Moody's pals Tad, Rob and Bob here. We're gonna be coming at you with another delightful comedy experience. When's a good time this morning to talk on the phone or Zoom?"

We talked. It was another Fox show. Called *Animal Control*, it chronicled the madcap lives of pest control officers in Seattle. It would shoot in Vancouver. Joel McHale would play the lead. I would play his nemesis, an uptight, rules-obsessed officer named Templeton Dudge. This was in August of 2022. By December, I was out west, hard at work, nose to the grindstone, toiling away, as always. I learned something from all of this. You can try and try and try to make something happen, but sometimes you just have to trust the process and trust yourself. I'm lucky to have been given the opportunities I have had, but I know it stems from two things: hard work and building relationships.

Oh, and not burning bridges. So, *three* things.

# PART THREE

Sports and Other Life Lessons

# THE COUNTRY CLUB EXPERIENCE

It was summertime, between Grades 6 and 7, and I was having a sleepover with my friend Alan. The next morning, Alan was going to go golfing with his older brother, James, and he asked me if I wanted to go. After pleading with my father, I went with the two brothers to a public course in the north end of Toronto called the Don Valley Golf Course. That day, my first ever as a golfer, I shot 136. If I'd counted all of my mulligans, and every time I moved my ball, I probably would have shot closer to 170.

Explaining why you love golf to someone who doesn't like it is difficult. Yes, it's slow. Yes, it's as frustrating as anything you'll ever do. But every once in a while, if only through sheer fluke, you *will* hit a good shot. You'll sink a long putt or drive the ball straight down the fairway. And then, for your efforts, you'll be graced with that glorious sense of accomplishment—that sense that the golf gods have looked down on you and said, "Okay, you know what? You're due." In that moment when the ball has actually done what you wanted it to do, you will feel as though all is well with the world. It doesn't last long. A few seconds at the most, and then you're on to the next shot. But I guarantee that when it does happen, you will want that feeling again. You will also imagine a round of golf filled with those moments of golfing bliss, and so you will want to get better. It's just what happens. I know, because it happened to me that day I went golfing with Alan and his brother James.

I think there was another reason I liked playing golf so much. Back then, I was a real video game kid. I loved Pac-Man, Galaga, Asteroids, you name it. I remember I bought a book on Pac-Man once and spent hours memorizing successful patterns. Today, I have a vintage Galaga machine at home, in my basement, which I still play from time to time. The thing I loved about video games was that, after playing, you got a score. You could try to beat that score the next time around. It was just you versus the game, and at the end of it, you received a number telling you how well you had done. Golf is like this. Other sports, not so much. Let's say I play a match in tennis. I do okay, but I want to play better the next time. So the next time, I do play better. My ground strokes land deeper and I hit a higher percentage of first serves. Yet, in this match, my opponent is a superior player. Though *I've* done better, it's not reflected in the result. With golf, there is an automatic relationship between how you did and the score you receive. If you play better, your score will improve. Your progress is objectively quantified, no matter who you're playing against. I found there was a comfort, and a simplicity, in this.

The next time I played, I shot a 128, which wasn't quite as bad as 136, though I did count more shots and took fewer mulligans. The next time, my score was a little better still, and I stayed even closer to playing by the rules.

You realize very quickly in golf that if you don't play by the rules, even when playing by yourself, you are just kidding yourself if you tell your friends what you shot. Most people who play golf recreationally don't play by the rules, because the fun is in beating your score. But I was super competitive, so I wanted my score to be real. Saying I broke a hundred when I took three mulligans means I didn't really break a hundred. I was hooked.

All I wanted to do was play golf, which was difficult, since I didn't belong to a club—there was no way my parents could ever afford it—and as a kid, it was incredibly difficult to get a tee time at public courses. Besides, you still had to pay. A round of golf at Don Valley cost about fifteen dollars back then. While this sounds like nothing, I still didn't have it. So I had a predicament: How could I play a sport I loved when I couldn't, in any way, afford to do so? Shortly thereafter, the gods of golf solved this problem in a way that I could never have expected: they delivered me to one of the best private clubs in the city.

But I'm getting ahead of myself. Around this time, I finished grade school and applied to De La Salle College in Toronto. While the school didn't have a golf program, it did have a yearly tournament for students. I did fairly well in that tournament and got to know some students in different grades whom I'd never met before. One of them mentioned that the Bayview Golf and Country Club had a program where they would allow kids to join whose parents couldn't afford the full membership dues.

I went home, excited. At dinner, I told the rest of my family what I'd learned. My sister said she had a friend named Beth Keaney, whose father was a member at Bayview. After dinner, she reached out to Beth and he agreed to sponsor me, meaning I could join Bayview, one of the most exclusive golf clubs in my area, for the princely sum of $150 a year. I was in.

That summer, I took the bus there, by myself, every day. I used a set of 1970 MacGregor clubs that belonged to my father and that were way too big for me. I didn't have golf shoes. I had a pair of old, torn golf gloves. I used golf balls that my friends and I fished out of the river that ran through the centre of the Don Valley course. And though I was happy to be there, I quickly learned that being a sponsored member was a little like carrying a sign around my neck that read "The Poor Kid." Now, I wouldn't say we were *poor*, since we had all the basic needs of life as a family. But to these rich folk at the club, I was held to a different standard. If you were caught breaking any rules, you were instantly kicked out. Any bad conduct at all, and you were out. One summer, a bunch of the men's lockers were broken into, the members' golf balls stolen. I was approached and asked if I had anything to do with it. I hadn't, of course, but the assumption was it must be the sponsored kid. They found out shortly after that it was a member's son, and he received a slap on the wrist.

And yet, regardless of the different way I was treated, I was delighted to be there. My father, who hadn't wanted me to play golf in the first place, would now say, "Gerry, you cannot blow this opportunity. Do you understand? You have to behave yourself."

I understood. I didn't know anybody there when I joined. I remember showing up the first day by myself, and a kid on the putting green named Peter Donato approached me and said, "Hey, you're the kid at De La Salle who I always see eating hash browns every day." I was—I loved the hash browns. Although we wouldn't play together there for a few weeks, it was nice to meet someone I kind of knew.

So, for the first few rounds, I played by myself. I started to get better. Taking lessons was never an option because we couldn't afford them, so instead, I would play as much as I could. Sometimes, I would go to the range and listen to the teaching pro, George Clifton, give lessons. I would hit balls beside him and his student and listen as much as I could. When a student would leave, George would always give me a few free tips while he waited for the next one.

One day, shortly after I joined, I was playing on a busy day. It must have been a Saturday or a Sunday. I was going into Grade 10 that summer, and I looked like I could've been going into Grade 6. On the fifteenth hole, I found myself stuck behind a slow foursome—one of the problems of playing alone is that you play very quickly. Meanwhile, there was a pair of older guys stuck behind me. They started yelling at me to hurry up. I answered with the refrain golfers use when they're held up by the golfers in front of them: "There's nowhere to go."

They pulled up just as the group in front of me was done the fifteenth hole. They told me they would be playing through. You usually *ask* to play through, but in this case, they *told* me they were, and as any golfer knows, singles are not welcome on the golf course. So off they went. By the time I got to the sixteenth hole, I found them waiting to hit. The group in front of them was indeed slow. I felt like saying, "Told ya," but, of course, that wasn't going to happen. To their credit, they said, "You're right, young man, there *is* nowhere to go. Why don't you join us for the last three holes?" So that's what I did.

We hit our balls off the seventeenth tee. It was a par three, 167 yards, pin tucked around the corner to the left, out of bounds on the left as well. I had played enough to know the hole very well. So I hit, and hit it well. A nice little draw to exactly where the pin was. We couldn't see the pin, but knew where it was. They were in a cart, so by the time I reached the green, they were already looking for my ball. I guessed I'd drawn it too much, so we started to look into the bushes on the left. We spent a few minutes doing that, and then they said, "Too bad, you hit that well. Just drop another one." I knew that wasn't the rule, but I wasn't going to head back to the tee to hit again. They went to their balls and started hitting their chips toward the hole. There was a part of me that thought maybe, just maybe, my ball was in the hole. But I certainly wasn't going to suggest that out loud. So I played my second ball onto the green. As one of the men started toward the hole to pull the pin out, I stared at the hole, wondering. Sure enough, he reached for the pin, and there it was: my orange Finalist, a ball I'd have scooped out of the river at Don Valley.

"That's my ball!" I exclaimed. "That's my ball!"

At the age of fourteen, five feet tall and eighty-five pounds, I had my first, and only, hole in one.

This changed my status considerably. The club gave everyone in the restaurant a free drink. The club gave me a dozen Titleist Balata balls, which were the finest—and most expensive—golf balls you could buy. It turned out that one of the old guys I'd golfed with was a friend of a newspaper reporter named George Gross. The next day, George put a snippet in the *Toronto Sun* sports section announcing the lucky feat. It was my proudest golf moment to date.

The head pro, a guy named Warren Crosbie, stopped calling me "kid" and started calling me "Ace." He also gave me a job as a caddy. For each round, I'd get fifty bucks. This led to caddying jobs for other members. Suddenly, I had a side hustle. Over the summers, I played, on average, 130 rounds of golf, mostly two rounds a day, every single day. People knew me. I was Ace, the kid who'd got the hole in one.

I got my handicap down to sixteen, then six, then two. At age seventeen, I played in the club championships and placed second behind the club's perennial champion, a guy named Mike Mealia. He had won the club title the past fifteen years straight. I felt at home now. And it wasn't just the golf—I was getting used to the lifestyle. I spent eight hours a day at Bayview. If there had been a bed there, I would have slept there. My mum and dad knew how much I loved it—when you're spending eight hours a day there, it means you're *eating* there for eight hours a day. It was easy to forget how much money my parents paid for my monthly food bills. But they never complained. Ever.

But at the end of the day, I'd have to go back to the real world, where money was always an issue. Looking back, I can tell you that at least ninety percent of my parents' arguments were about money—which bill to pay first, which kid *really* needed a new winter coat, whether the car could go another year without falling apart. At Bayview, it was different. There, the stress caused by financial problems didn't exist. Everyone had everything they wanted, when they wanted it. That's when I decided that, one day, I wanted to become as successful as them—and by successful, I meant having money. I just knew that having no money was way, way, *way* worse than being rich.

That year, I qualified for the Ontario Junior Golf Championships, which were played at the Chedoke Golf Club in Hamilton. Based on my performance at the Ontario juniors, I qualified for the Canadian juniors, which were to be held at the Windermere Golf and Country Club in Edmonton.

I went to see Mr. Crosbie.

"Can I talk to you?"

"Sure, Ace."

"Sir, I qualified for the Canadian Junior Championship."

"I heard."

"It's in Edmonton."

"I know that."

"The thing is . . . well . . . my father's a bus driver. My mother stays home. They can't afford to send me there, so I was wondering . . . is there any way, you know, that the club could sponsor me?"

He looked straight at me and blinked.

"Yeah," he said, before walking off.

It was my first time on a plane. The club (or Mr. Crosbie—I don't really know) paid for everything: my flight, my hotel, my meals. I showed up at the course and suddenly realized what a big deal this was: TSN was covering the event. I placed forty-ninth. Mike Weir finished seventh. I'd never had so much fun.

In Grade 13, I started working at The Keg. Though I still golfed, I couldn't get to the club as often as I used to. When I turned nineteen and my sponsorship ended, Warren Crosbie hired me to work in the back shop. The transition from one of the best players at the club to the back shop didn't work out for me. I was too comfortable with the members, and vice versa. Mr. Crosbie didn't like that the members treated me differently than the other back shoppers; it didn't look good. There was nothing I could do.

I didn't play golf for another ten years. One day, I was watching the Masters in 1999, when I suddenly realized something: I missed golf. I tried to play a few times and didn't enjoy it. After being spoiled playing at Bayview, I now had to resort to waiting hours to play at public courses. This inspired an examination of my life. A decade earlier, while drinking a milkshake on the course at Bayview, I had promised myself I'd either become wealthy or die trying. Now I was a teacher. Despite having two university degrees, I lived in a small apartment, drove a crappy car and was still drowning in debt. People told me I was funny. One of my students had even suggested I try stand-up. Could I actually make money—*real* money—as a comedian? I decided to give it a shot. If nothing else, Bayview gave me this determination.

When I was forty and had a bit of money, I went back to the Bayview and took out a family membership. Though I did play, I didn't do it very often; for some reason, my days as a junior couldn't ever be matched. I kept the membership for nearly fifteen years, but only because my daughter Aly had developed the same passion for golf that I had. Aly got really good. She made some good friends there, just like I did. Then two of her friends left for a club closer to their home. Another two moved to the States to pursue golf fulltime. Suddenly, she didn't have her friends to play with, and that changed everything. I was a member at another club by this time as well, and since Aly had left golf, it didn't make sense to stay at Bayview.

I just left Bayview a few months ago. I have so many great memories of the place, and in many ways, it shaped my goals and dreams. I met so many great people there. I still talk to Warren Crosbie once in a while. He was a great pro to me when I was younger, and I learned a lot from him. The same goes for Doug Rankin, Bob Lane and Terry Kirkup, who were all assistant pros when I was a junior there. They would sit and talk to me in the pro shop for hours—about golf and about life. I always thought my kids would love it there as much as I did, but it never happened because they didn't connect to golf to the same extent that I did. Maybe one day they will.

Thanks for the memories, Bayview Golf and Country Club. Those were some of the best days of my life.

# SCHOOL

**M**y parents never involved themselves that intensely when it came to my education. They cared and checked in, but they really only got concerned when they saw me failing something, which rarely happened. Though they knew I went to school, they wouldn't have known what courses I was taking. It didn't matter to my parents whether I did well on a test or bombed on a test, for the simple reason that they would never, ever have known about the test in the first place. The only time I ever heard from them was the day I brought home my report card. If I was failing at something, my father would tell me to smarten up. So I learned quickly that, as long as I didn't screw up totally, I'd be fine. This belief carried me through most of my academic career.

The truth is that I was never wild about school. I'm not the sort of person who can just sit still behind a desk and absorb information. It doesn't work that way for me. I finished high school with an average of sixty-nine. While this wasn't particularly good, I hadn't failed, so it was fine with my parents. I then applied to university. I don't know how it works now, but back then, you could apply to three universities in Ontario. I had a lot of friends who were going to Western, so that was my first pick. My second was King's University College *at* Western. My third choice was York University, which I didn't really want to go to at all, and only applied to because I felt like I had to put down something.

York was the only one of the three to accept me. So I had to decide: go to York, or take a year off, save a little money, apply to another round of universities next year and hope to get into a school I actually wanted to attend.

I told my father about my conundrum. He promptly made a list of pros and cons. On the pro side for going to York, he had three entries:

1. My sister was about to have a baby. If I stayed in Toronto, I'd be closer to my niece.
2. I could keep my job at The Keg, which would help pay for my tuition.
3. I could save tons of money by living at home.

Meanwhile, I supplied the only entry on the cons side: I wanted to go away to university. My brother had gone away to university. I wanted to follow in his footsteps.

I went to York.

It was an hour each way by bus. I had already been commuting to high school for five years. I also had no social life. I remember I did a lot of waiting around—I'd have a class at ten in the morning, and another at four in the afternoon. *What*, I was constantly asking myself, *was I going to do between the two of them?* I was studying business, which I hated. On top of everything else, I was lazy. I missed most of my morning classes. There were classes I never went to— not even once—only to drop the course just before it would count on my transcript. It was easy. All you had to do was phone a number at York and punch in the number of the course you wanted to stop taking. So I did this all the time. I'd quit a course in the morning, select another course by the afternoon, and change my mind by the end of the week, at which point I'd phone the cancellation line to get some of my money back. The sooner I dropped the course, the more money I got back.

I switched my major to geography. Why, I'm not sure—I suppose because geography was as far from business as anything else I could think of. Then I got it into my head that I'd be a doctor. I took chemistry and physics, only to discover that chemistry and physics were really, really hard, particularly when you hadn't taken them in high school.

By the end of my first year, I had exactly three credits. The first was Anatomy of Advertising, a business course I'd never gotten around to quitting. The second was called Science and Environment, which was a holdover from my months as a geography student. It was one of the classes I never went to once—the exam, for me, was guesswork. I had a half credit in calculus, which was the lone pre-med course I actually completed. I also had a half credit in another business course called Principles of Economics 1. So that's where I was at the end of eight months—three lousy credits, spread over as many disciplines. My best mark was in calculus—I got a C-plus.

I came to realize that I wasn't motivated. I wasn't taking courses I liked, and I had no idea what I wanted to do as a career. University felt like a job that I hated, except instead of getting a paycheque every week, I paid them to work. It just wasn't for me.

I went to Mexico with a friend of mine. There, we hung out with a bunch of students from Wilfrid Laurier, who all seemed to love going there. When I got home, I immediately applied to transfer there. A month or two later, I got a letter from the school saying that while they'd take me, they wouldn't accept my credits from York, and I'd have to start all over again. I decided to go anyway. I made it all the way to the mailbox, and was about to send a confirmation that I was coming, when it hit me. If I transferred to Wilfrid Laurier, my whole first year would have been for nothing.

So I didn't go. I figured I'd stick it out at York, no matter how much I hated it. That summer, I happened to run into my golf buddy Peter Donato, who, coincidentally, also went to York. I told him how much I hated commuting from home. He grinned.

"Gerry," he said, "me and two buddies have a quad in residence."

"Oh," I said.

"We need another guy. Why don't *you* be the fourth?"

I went home and told my father. He was confused, and more than a little bit angry. "Why on *earth*," he asked, "would you pay to live in residence when you already have a place to stay in Toronto?"

I had no answer. My brother, who was home for the summer, did. "Dad," he said, "it's not an education unless you move away! It teaches you how to cook for yourself, how to do your laundry, how to manage your whole life." There was a pause. My father didn't say anything. He was either fuming or reconsidering. In the end, he agreed with Kevin, and off I went.

Living in residence, if I still did poorly at school, it was for a different reason altogether. I was now having too much fun. I acquired a circle of friends. I got my first girlfriend. I played more intramural sports, for the simple reason that it was now way easier to get to them. I clearly remember going to the pub, coming home at 2 a.m., and then starting to study for an exam I had the next day. Though my average crept up slightly from first year, I was still a solid C-plus student at best.

So, what did I do? I applied to law school. I'm not sure exactly why. Perhaps I'd heard it was something a student with two years of a general arts program under his or her belt could do. Nobody would take me. My marks were terrible. I didn't study for the Law School Admission Test (LSAT), and I scored in the forty-ninth percentile. There was this guy in the exam hall whose pager kept going off during the exam. In the absence of anything better, I'll blame my dismal performance on him and my ADHD. But applying to law school was a good thing. It meant I was maturing and starting to think about a career. After all, that's why you went to university, right? On top of that, I was a little embarrassed by how stupid I felt about bombing the LSAT. It was time to take it up a notch.

For my third year, I transferred into kinesiology. I can still remember the courses I took: Intro to Computers, Basic Gymnastics, Basic Movement, History of Physical Education, Fitness Assessment, anatomy, biomechanics, statistics, psychology and sociology. Of these, the hardest by far was statistics. Yet I got an A-plus. Somehow, I just got it—I think it was from all of the sports statistics I'd memorized. One of the courses I enjoyed was an elective called Women and Society. Why would I take this course? Simple: everyone told me that only women took it. Sure enough, I was the only man in a room with fifteen other women. I had expected this. Having come from an all-boys high school, not only was it a good idea to take this course, but I *needed* to take it. Prior to that course, I'd never heard the word *patriarchal*. It had never occurred to me how much more opportunity I'd had because of my gender. I never knew how frustrated women were with the way our culture worked. Having come from the chauvinistic world of sports, I was now a feminist in training.

If I worked harder in third year, it was likely because I had a game plan. Once again, I was thinking I might apply to med school. I figured that, with all of my anatomy courses, I knew the human body better than most of the science students who were applying. Yet I also knew that you needed extremely high marks to get into medical school. So I had a fallback: if I didn't get into medical school, I'd apply to teacher's college. With a plan in place, I studied hard, recorded all of my lectures, went to all of my classes and prepared for my exams. My average was now A-minus. I needed a fifth year to catch up on all the credits I'd missed during my first two years, and my average in that fifth year was a solid A. All in all, I could have probably put a down payment on a house with the money I had lost dropping courses over the years. But at least I'd found my way. I would become a doctor. Maybe cure a disease. Lyme disease would be at the top of that list.

I applied to the medical school program at McMaster University in Hamilton. It was the only school that didn't make you write the Medical College Admission Test (MCAT), and it was also pretty lenient when it came to science course requirements. Yet I still had two things working against me: my bad grades during my first two years, and the application. I'd expected something similar to the application forms I'd filled out when applying to Western and York. Instead, I had to write a multi-page biographical essay. This was a challenge. I'm just not a writerly guy. I confess that in my life, I've read exactly four books. One was a biography of Wayne Gretzky. One was about Jim Carrey. One was the life of Michael J. Fox. The last was a book called *Tuesdays with Morrie*. I have now written exactly half as many books as I have read. Pretty good ratio—my stats class taught me that. And now I had to write my way into medical school. In addition to that big essay, there were twenty-two other short essays, all demanding one-to-two-hundred word answers, on such topics as team-working abilities, self-directed learning, ethical sensitivity, leadership abilities . . . the list went on and on. For a question regarding curiosity and creativity, I put down that I was really, really good at lip-synching. At the time, I thought this was probably exactly the sort of thing they were looking for.

I finished the application and sent it off. I must confess, I really enjoyed applying to medical school. People would come up to me and say, "So, Gerry, what are you doing next year?"

"Probably going to med school."

"Really?"

"Oh, yeah." I'd shrug, as if this were no more impressive than crossing the street. "I'm just waiting to hear back."

"Where did you apply?"

"McMaster."

"Anywhere else?"

"No . . . not really. I just really like the program at McMaster. It seems so much more open-minded. More of a self-directed learning approach, which better suits me. You know, they really value all of your life experiences there."

I was shocked when I didn't get in. If you saw the application, I'm sure you'd know why. Someone, somewhere in the world read that application and laughed. A lot.

I started applying to teacher's colleges, only to discover that they were almost as hard to get into as med school. I applied everywhere: York, the University of Toronto, the University of British Columbia, the University of Saskatchewan, Lakehead, Nipissing, Brock and Queen's. There were sixteen teacher's colleges in Canada, and I applied to each one of them. Each one, in turn, rejected me. I started looking at colleges in the United States, even though they would have been way too expensive for me. No matter. I was seriously looking at a master's program in athletic therapy at the University of Indiana, solely because it was only a one-year program. I figured that if I got in, I'd go, and worry about money later.

But then, one day, I heard about a little school in Antigonish, Nova Scotia, called St. Francis Xavier University. It had an odd academic quirk: those who graduated with a physical education degree at St. FX were automatically given a teacher's certificate by the government of Nova Scotia. It was a concurrent program. Suddenly, I had an idea. Even though I *already* had a phys. ed. degree from York, I'd see if I could transfer into the phys. ed. program at St. FX. I looked into it. It turned out they wouldn't accept some of my York credits, but they accepted enough that, if I transferred, I could start in my third year. This, I figured, was destiny: in two years, I could get my teacher's certificate.

So I applied. Shortly afterward, I got a telephone call from an admissions officer at St. FX. She told me that I had a decent application. There was, however, a problem. They only accepted four transfers into the phys. ed. program each year. And this included transfers from within the school. Yet another problem: they gave preference to those transferring from within the school. Still another problem: I wasn't the only student who'd found out that the St. FX physical education program was a way of gaming your way into the teaching profession.

"I'm sorry," she said. "Your application really was quite good. It's just that we've reached our quota. I'm sorry."

She hung up. I remember sitting on the end of the bed, feeling as low as I'd ever felt. That week, Indiana had told me I would need to do two years if they even considered me. Now I was truly out of options. What would I do? Wait tables and reapply next year? I couldn't move for a half-hour. And then, the phone rang. It was the admissions officer from St. FX again. She told me that she'd felt bad after we'd spoken. She also said that they'd reviewed my application one more time and decided that, this year only, they'd make an exception and take one more transfer student.

"By any chance," she asked me, "would you still be interested?"

"Yes," I told her, "I would."

So, there it was. I got into St. FX, became a teacher, and then became a comic who told funny stories about having been a teacher. Looking back, it often feels like the course of my life was determined by that half-hour I spent sitting on the edge of my bed, feeling as though there was nothing in store for me. But then the phone rang, and everything changed. Life, I think, is like that.

Now I have three kids, all of whom are in school. Aly and Faith are a little like me—they find it boring to just sit and learn. Breton, meanwhile, is more like his mother. Heather was the sort of student who never got a mark below ninety. Not surprisingly, her parents were completely unlike mine. If she got a ninety-eight on an exam, her mother would ask her one thing and one thing only: Which question did you get wrong?

Naturally, she's like this with our kids. I, however, am more like my parents. When it comes to grades, I'm just not that interested. For me, it's more important that my kids are interesting and have manners. Of course, Heather wants that, too, but she is also concerned about marks, and I totally understand why. The best thing you can do for children, I figure, is let them find their own way.

The other day, Faith came home with a seventy-five on a test. Heather was not pleased. She wanted to meet with the teacher, to establish a study regimen, to *really* get at the heart of the problem. So we compromised. Heather wasn't wrong, and neither was I. One thing I tell all my kids is to find something they are passionate about and chase it as hard and as long as they can. That's what I did, and it's worked out well so far. Except for applying to medical school. And law school. Those didn't work out too well. Lyme disease still doesn't have a cure, by the way. Just sayin'.

# HOCKEY, HOCKEY, HOCKEY

When I was six, I started playing hockey in the local church league. All of the team names were highly Catholic. I started on Blessed Trinity, before advancing to St. Gabriel's and, a little later, St. Timothy's. I still remember my first goal playing for the mighty "BT." (I'm not sure if the Father, the Son and the Holy Spirit would have approved of that nickname, but ignorance is bliss, as they say.) There was a loose puck in the slot. I walked up on my skates and shovelled it into the net. I raised my stick in the air, just like they did on *Hockey Night in Canada*, at which point I also got my very first penalty: two minutes for raising my stick over my head. It was a stupid rule.

I sat in the penalty box, a big smile on my face. I also remember thinking my teammates would make a big deal of my goal when I got back to the bench. Yet, by the time my two minutes were up, none of my teammates seemed to remember what had happened. I didn't even get to keep the puck, since it belonged to one of the kids on the team. That's house league for you.

I remember walking up the church aisle at mass the next day to receive communion, thinking I was a big deal. I had just scored the game-winning goal against St. Bonaventure the night before. I assumed they were our rival. But I wasn't a big deal. They weren't our rival. I guess all the saints get along. And the church league results weren't on the radar of the parishioners. Oh, well. They should be. If you're going to name a team after the Blessed Trinity, at least act interested in the team's success. Notre Dame University sure does.

It was the only goal I scored that year. Still, I persevered. By my third year in the league, I got asked to play on the select team, which was made up of all the best players from the church league. The team was called the Knights of Columbus, and we played select teams from other leagues across the city. Though I'd gotten much better, I wasn't close to being the best player on the team, an honour belonging to a guy named Gerry Ronan. This, of course, led to confusion. I can't tell you how many times I heard our coach yell, "Get out there, Gerry!" Then, as I was leaping over the boards, I'd feel a hand grab my jersey and pull me back in. "Not *you*," the coach would yell. "The other Gerry, Gerry."

At the age of fourteen, I quit the church league, mostly because I had started high school and the school I went to had its own rink and plenty of hockey. Also, my mum didn't drive and my dad worked shifts, so it was a lot easier on everyone. Instead, I played high school intramural hockey, which was cheaper and easier to get to. I did well enough that I was asked to play on the school bantam team, which was basically made up of the best ninth-graders from the intramural league who couldn't make the junior team. I made the move, establishing a pattern that has existed for my entire life: while I was better than average, I wasn't good enough to be considered really good, if that makes any sense. In Grade 10, I did make the junior team, though as a third-line player. In Grade 11, I got cut from that same junior team, only to make it again in Grade 12—since I was born in December, I was still eligible to play on the junior team with mostly Grade 9 and 10 players. These included Kris Draper, Shane Bowler and Sean McCann, who were all in Grade 9 and were all far, far better than me: Sean went on to become the captain at Harvard and play professionally in the American Hockey League and International Hockey League for eight years. Shane led the team in scoring at the University of Alabama-Huntsville, and Kris went on to play over a thousand games in the NHL and win four Stanley Cups. So, yes, they were all better than me, even though they were three years younger.

In Grade 13, I didn't play at all and probably wouldn't have made the senior team anyway. I was a very average student, and I think I wanted to focus on my schoolwork so that I might actually get into university.

When I started at York University, there were two intramural leagues. One was full-contact, while the other was non-contact. The best players joined the contact league. I played in the non-contact league and had a lot of points. Keep in mind, anyone could play on the team, so it wasn't that hard for me. A friend in residence suggested I join the contact league the following year, so I tried out for our residence team and made it. We were called the Bethune Dragons. We had team jackets, and yes, I wore mine, even though I played on the fourth line and barely saw any ice time. By my fourth year, I had moved up to the second line. By my fifth year, I'd made it to the top line, which surprised no one more than me. But let's remember, it was still university intramurals and York University's varsity team were the current national champions. Meaning nobody cared about us.

That year, I got accepted to St. FX in Antigonish. I had this idea to try to make the university team out there. Another stupid idea, I guess, but I really wanted to try. The late bloomer in me thought I had a chance.

I spent that summer working out and Rollerblading everywhere I went. I was in the best shape of my life that September, when I arrived at tryouts. At this point, I started to have doubts—the St. FX team had guys who had played in the Quebec Major Junior Hockey League, the Ontario Hockey League and the Western Hockey League, all of which were spawning grounds for actual NHL players. There were players who—and I am not making this up—had gone to actual NHL camps. Every single one of them had experience playing, at a minimum, Junior B. What had I done? Church league hockey. Intramural hockey. Say what you will about me, but I am nothing if not determined.

I showed up on the first day weighing all of 155 pounds. I wore these huge Donzi shoulder pads to try to make myself look bigger. Instead, they made me look like a small guy trying to look bigger. My skates were still the same pair I'd worn playing intramural at York. As I got changed in the dressing room, I talked to nobody, for the simple reason that I didn't know anybody. It was intimidating. The team's top players were Dan LeBlanc, Duane Saulnier, Doug Synishin and Peter Lisy. All had played in the Ontario Hockey League. Fortunately, I didn't know who any of them were, as none of them had played in my church league growing up. So I stayed. I wasn't even sure if there were any spots open on the team, but I went out on the ice with my outdated stick and skates and gave it my all.

After all that Rollerblading, it took me about half an hour to get my footing and balance. Once I did, I started to feel okay, even though players who were much larger than I was were trying to crush me. I'd never seen such fierce hitting, and this was at a *tryout*. Still, all my training paid off. If anything kept me alive that day, it was my cardio strength. While I wasn't the best out there, I wasn't the worst. Or, at least, I didn't think so. The last skate was a blue-and-white scrimmage. Flukishly, I did well.

The next day, I walked over to the athletic centre, knowing that the list of players who had made the cut would be posted. As I approached the building, I felt good. While I probably hadn't been picked—the odds were just too long— I was proud that I had, at the very least, given it a shot. I stepped into the building, and at the end of the hall, I saw a

171

few people huddled around a list. My heart raced as I neared. I stood in front of it, peering over the shoulders of some phys. ed. students, and saw my name, Gerry Donoghue.

Somehow, it was *there*. I felt like Rudy from Notre Dame.

A few days later, I went to my first practice, at which point things got weirder still. I walked into the dressing room, where the lines were posted on a whiteboard. I'd be the centre on a line that included the team captain, Dan LeBlanc, and a local star from the Antigonish Bulldogs Junior A team named Dave MacNeil. They also put me on the first power-play unit. It was like I'd been blasted into some alternate universe, one in which people who weren't quite good enough suddenly became more than good enough. My brain fumbled for an explanation. Had I really done that well in tryouts? Or was this the worst team in the history of St. FX hockey? Neither theory, I have to say, could explain what I was doing there. I didn't know systems. I didn't know what to do on a draw. I didn't know anything about positioning. And I certainly didn't have a clue what I was doing on breakouts. But beside my stall were two brand new sticks and a brand new pair of skates.

My first game was an exhibition against St. Mary's University. On my third shift, I tried to hit a guy and separated my shoulder. I was out for the first three road games of the season. *Here I go again*, I thought. *My descent into mediocrity*. But no! For the home opener, the coach once again had me on the first line to start the game. I remember standing at centre ice during the national anthem. That's when it hit me: I'd never been on the ice for a national anthem. The closest I'd come were the prayers we said before hitting the ice in the church league.

We were playing the University of Prince Edward Island. One of their players, John Nelson, had played for the Toronto Marlboros in the OHL; he was drafted in the tenth round of the 1989 NHL Entry Draft. I remember every moment of that game. We won, 4–3. I scored with two minutes left to break a 3–3 tie, after assisting on the other three goals. I was named player of the game. I should have quit right then and there.

So, what had happened? A fluke? An act of God? Some collective hallucination that, in the real world, never happened at all? All I know is that everything went downhill from there. By Christmas I was on the fourth line. One day, after Christmas, the coach suggested I watch a tape of the first game, the insinuation being that I might figure out what I had been doing then that I wasn't doing now. I went home, turned on the tape and saw a bunch of tall guys in shorts—apparently, the basketball coach had got hold of the tape and recorded over it. I ended the season with ten points and didn't make the team the next year. So, there it was: my hockey-playing career was over. I'd started on teams named after saints, and I'd ended on a team named after a saint. It all seemed so fitting. Amen.

It's been exactly thirty years since that glorious first university game. I still talk about it with Dan, Duane and Doug, as we are all still friends. They laugh at how good I was in that one game, and how bad I was in the other twenty-two. I just keep talking about that one game. They keep talking about the other twenty-two. Playing that year was one of the highlights of my life. That game was something I think about often. *Too* often, my kids tell me.

I surprised myself in so many ways. Years later, I would use this experience in my comedy career. If I wanted to achieve something, I knew that hard work was the answer, along with an undeniable belief that you can do it. When I told people I wanted to make that team, they told me I didn't have a chance. It was the same thing people told me when I said I wanted to become a comedian at the age of thirty. To my mind, there's no such thing as "no chance" if you believe in "chance." I did, and it paid off. I still have my jacket, I still have my jersey and I still have the puck from that first goal in university. But I am still missing the puck from my very first goal in hockey as a kid. If anyone has the game puck from October 21, 1975, Blessed Trinity vs. St. Bonaventure at Don Mills Arena in Toronto, please contact me. I need it to bookend my two biggest goals.

After St. FX, I returned to Toronto, teaching diploma in hand, and did my placement teaching—sort of the educational equivalent of articling—at St. Robert Catholic School in North York. At night, I moonlighted at one of two jobs: I was a waiter at a local Keg restaurant, and later became a bartender at a bar downtown called Crocodile Rock.

One night, when I was working at The Keg, the principal from St. Robert's, named Gerry Brand—yes, another Gerry—was sitting in my section. He knew the principal at

De La Salle, and he told me they were hiring immediately because one of the teachers wasn't working out. So I applied. Being an alumnus helped. I met with the principal a few days later.

"Gerry," I remember her asking me. "Could you teach history?"

"A hundred percent," I said. I knew nothing about history.

"And your computer skills are good?"

"For sure." They didn't exist.

"Well, then," she said, "can you start in two days?"

I feverishly read up on history before teaching the curriculum the next day. My cluelessness, in fact, influenced my creation of the Mr. D character, the only difference being that Mr. D the television character didn't know how dumb he was, whereas I went to great lengths to hide my ignorance. Often, I'd ask a question to my class and have no idea what the answer was, as I'd gotten home too late from my waitering job to read the chapters I'd assigned the day before. Usually, I'd let one of the smart kids answer. Then I'd nod my head and say, "Yep, that's pretty much it. Anyone have any questions?"

When I started at De La Salle, I did three things right away. The first was to get rid of the previous teacher's pet rock, which he kept as some sort of hokey class mascot. The second was to restore order in the class; under the previous teacher, it had gotten completely out of control, and I told the kids I wouldn't stand for it. The third, however, was by far my biggest project. I decided to restore the school's hockey program.

Years earlier, De La Salle had one of the better high school hockey teams in the Greater Toronto Area. Keanu Reeves had played net (he was good). The team also provided a training ground for such NHL players as Kris Draper, Richard Park, Bill Bowler and Eddie Shack. In 1994, De La Salle went private, and that year it had a student body of about two hundred. Many programs were cut, including hockey.

By the time I got there, enrolment had grown to about four hundred kids. I figured it was time that the team came back to life. So, I coached after school. We started doing well, defeating the teams at Upper Canada College and St. Mike's. Sometime toward the end of the season, one of the kids' fathers said he wanted to talk to me. Apparently, he was the accountant for Brett Callighen, an ex-professional hockey player who had the distinction of playing on Wayne Gretzky's line with the Edmonton Oilers. Callighen, he told me, was now running a school called the Hockey Institute and was looking for instructors. I talked to Brett, and he hired me on the spot.

This, then, was my routine. First, I'd teach all day. After school, I'd coach the De La Salle hockey team. Then I'd drive across town and give an hour-long drills class for the Hockey Institute, for which I was paid all of fifteen dollars. Then, I'd go to my restaurant job. It was no wonder the students in my class often knew the subject material better than me—I had no time to learn it. Then, I'd wake up the next morning and do it all over again.

But I'm like that. I take on too much. I think of it as sweat equity: if you put yourself out there, things come to you. In my second year of coaching De La Salle, I was approached by two parents who asked me to coach the Don Mills Flyers AAA team that both of their ten-year-old sons were on.

It was a quick conversation.

"We'll give you twenty thousand dollars," they said.

"Done," I said.

It was becoming common practice in AA and AAA hockey: you want a good coach, you pay them. At that level, a team can easily have two games and three practices a week, so it was a huge commitment.

Now, in addition to coaching at De La Salle and teaching at the Hockey Institute, I was the head coach of the Don Mills Flyers, the same AAA team Leafs superstar Mitch Marner would later play for. To make time in my schedule, I quit my restaurant job, which I didn't need since I was twenty thousand dollars richer. I now had my foot in the door coaching AAA hockey, and I loved it.

It wasn't long before I was offered a coaching job with another AAA team, the Wexford Raiders. This time, there was no money. I didn't care; I coached for the love of it. There's something about guiding young players, not just in sports but in life, that I found gratifying. Back at De La Salle, I had access to the players' grades, and if a kid wasn't doing well, I'd bench them. I remember saying to one kid, "You're getting a thirty in English? You're not playing today." Though he didn't like it, his grades sure improved quickly.

But, if you ask any coach to name the biggest challenge they face coaching elite athletes, they will all tell you: it's the parents. As I coached, I quickly learned that these parents want it so badly for their kids. Some see the NHL as a possibility, even though the odds are stacked against even the good AAA players. It was sometimes comical how focused parents were on their kids becoming a professional hockey player. You often have conversations like this as a coach:

> **Parent:** My son is pretty good, isn't he?
> **Coach:** He is. Excellent skater. Good little player.
> **Parent:** He wants to play in the NHL bad. Think he has a chance?
> **Coach:** Maybe, but it's so early to tell because he's *seven years old*!

After my first three games with the Raiders, our record was one win, two losses. This, I thought, was respectable, given that I was new and the team needed to grow into some changes I'd made. Even if we'd been 0 and 3, I'd have been happy with the way the team was starting to come together. The parents, however, weren't. They told me they wanted a meeting. It happened in a vacant dressing room. The more vocal among them wanted to know why the team wasn't winning. All I could say were the sort of things that coaches always say when defending a less-than-stellar record: don't worry, it takes time, there've been a lot of changes, we've got a great bunch of young players. It felt ridiculous to have to say this about a team made up of ten-year-olds, but there I was, saying, "Don't worry, we'll get there. I know we will."

One of the more belligerent parents stood up. He was upset because I had agreed I wouldn't have any parents on the bench in a coaching role. But I did need to have a certified trainer on the bench, and they were hard to find. One of our parents was a paramedic, and he accepted the role. So I had him on the bench out of necessity. He was great at it.

"This is *bullshit*," said the parent. "You said no parents on the bench." He then pointed at my trainer and yelled, "Then why is *he* on the bench?" My trainer looked at his shoes. I looked at the seething father.

"Don't worry," I said. "You won't have to see him on the bench again."

"Good."

"You won't have to see him because I will be releasing your son tomorrow. I won't tolerate anyone talking to my staff that way." The room went silent, and I mean silent.

He stormed out, and the kid was playing for another team the next day.

A couple of nights after that, I got a call from another parent. I'll call him Larry.

"Hallo, Gerry?" he mumbled.

"Yes."

"Izz Larry."

"Larry. It's eleven o'clock at night."

"I knowizz eleven, so what?"

"Larry. Have you been drinking?"

"Maybe a few, sowhattaguy can't have a beerortwo?"

"Larry, what is it?"

"Whazz this one and two shit?"

179

"Larry, seriously, we are three games in and you are calling me at 11 p.m. on a Tuesday night?"

"It's bullshit, Gerry. You said this team would be good. Yer an asshole, you know that?"

"Seriously, Larry? I'm writing all of this down."

"Yer what?"

"I'm writing this down."

"You're taking notes, are you? Look at you, ya little lawyer."

"Larry. You just called me an asshole."

"I did?"

"You did."

There was a pause.

"Did you check your notes?"

That made me laugh out loud. He started laughing as well, and the call ended in a very civil manner. I realized something after that call, something that I still see this day when I'm around my own kids and their sports. When the parents get desperate for their kid to "make it," the desperation makes them say and do desperate things. And desperate parents are never a good thing.

I left the Raiders five games before the end of season. The parents grouped together and fired me from a job for which I wasn't getting paid. One of the parents took over, and the team fell apart the next year, as many AAA hockey teams do. A few days later, I got a call from the guy who owned all of the Wexford teams. He told me he needed an assistant coach on the Wexford Junior A team. I'd be the second assistant. The head coach was Kevin Burkett, who was very well respected in the Toronto area. I said yes, and worked for him during the 1997 and 1998 seasons. I learned a lot from him during that time.

Meanwhile, through all of this, I was still coaching at De La Salle and working at the Hockey Institute. In 1999, Brett Callighen asked me if I wanted to buy the school and take it over so that he could focus on the player agency he had built in Europe. I really liked this idea and jumped at the opportunity.

"How much?" I asked.

"How about twenty thousand?"

"Done," I said, and that was it. We never signed anything, and he told me I could take as long as I wanted to pay down the twenty thousand. He went off to Europe, and I had myself a hockey school. At nights and during school breaks, I'd run hockey clinics. Soon, I was hiring other coaches to run the clinics to grow the school. I quickly discovered that, as much as I loved coaching hockey, I loved owning a small business even more. After a year or so, I met with a parent from De La Salle who was the CEO of PepsiCo Canada and managed to acquire a sponsor for a program I had in mind, in which I'd find the best young players in Toronto and invite them to a hockey skills camp. Never shy about hyperbole, I called it the Pepsi Elite Excellence Program. Over the five years I ran it, we had players like Steven Stamkos, John Tavares, P.K. Subban, Jeff Skinner and Connor Brown. My brother was a huge help in running it with me and arranging to find the players, since he was coaching AAA more than I was. Years later, when I started doing "Gerry Dee, Sports Reporter," I got interviews that legitimate sports reporters couldn't get, because a lot of the players remembered me from my days running the Pepsi camp.

Coaching and teaching hockey would be my future. It was my passion. I was determined to pursue it as a full-time job, and hoped to one day coach junior, college or professional hockey. There was just one obstacle: I had become obsessed with stand-up comedy. It quickly became the only thing I wanted to do. In 2002, a parent who was very involved in minor hockey asked me if I had any interest in selling the hockey school. I didn't know him too well, but I knew he was a good guy and also knew that money wasn't an issue for him.

"You know," I told him, "I just might."

"Tell you what," he said. "Why don't we just meet for breakfast and talk about it? We don't have to make any decisions now."

The very next morning, we met for breakfast at a restaurant near De La Salle. We sat. We ordered. Before the food came, he reached into a satchel he was carrying and placed a brown paper bag in the middle of the table.

"What's that?" I asked.

"That," he said, "is fifty thousand dollars to purchase your hockey school."

I looked at it, amazed. I didn't even really know what he was paying for. Essentially, *I* was the hockey school. I guess he was paying for the name, the database and access to my instructors, but I wasn't going to ask a lot of questions with a bag full of money sitting in front of me. It felt like a drug deal, but it was just a hockey school deal.

I took it. I was now out of coaching hockey. About a year later, I quit my job at De La Salle and became a full-time comedian. I didn't coach hockey again for almost twenty years, when I became the coach of my son's team in the exact same church league where I had first played hockey. My son was not one of the best players, but luckily, everyone got to play. He didn't love hockey, and he only played for one year, but we both knew his heart wasn't really in it. And, yes, I was disappointed—I had never imagined that my son *wouldn't* play hockey. I tried putting my daughters into it as well; they preferred volleyball, which competed in the same season.

When my son quit, I was a little relieved. Hockey can be a tough sport to watch your own kid play; I was always afraid that he'd go headfirst into the boards. I suppose what I'm most upset about is that he won't have those dressing room experiences. In hockey, it's all about the camaraderie. Ask any retired hockey player what they miss the most, and they'll tell you it's the locker room. Instead, my son chose volleyball. Like his sisters. He's really good. But what really matters is that he loves it and he's learning that effort, diligence and teamwork all pay off.

It is January 1, 2023, as I'm writing this. Halfway through typing this chapter, I got a text from Bill Markle wishing me a happy New Year. Bill was one of my first coaches from my church league days. We've kept in touch all these years, as he is also a De La Salle alumnus. Bill is in his eighties now. He's smart as a whip and as nice as they get. I couldn't have asked for a better coach in my first years of hockey. That's one of the best parts of hockey: the friendships you make. I still keep in touch with lots of players from over the years, and it doesn't matter if you played house league, intramurals or university. It is the best part of the game.

I hope volleyball does the same thing for my kids. I'm pretty sure it will.

# HARD KNOCKS

The year was 1999, and I'd been teaching at De La Salle for three years. Every fall, the school hosted a fund-raising day; each homeroom came up with a way of raising money for ShareLife, a Catholic charity that gives money to a wide range of social service agencies. Typically, there were bake sales, pizza sales and hot dog sales. You had a jelly-bean count, a balloon-popping contest and a floor hockey game in which you got to play for a dollar. You could pay a couple of bucks to throw a pie at a teacher's face. The previous year, I'd been one of the teachers who volunteered for the dunk tank. Unfortunately, I took my turn at the end of the day, when the water was filthy. I sat on the perch, only to plunge into the tank whenever a kid hit the bull's eye with a softball. The students would all laugh and I'd climb back onto the perch. Again, and again, and again. The next day, I came down with pink eye. We raised forty-two dollars.

This year, I wanted to come up with something really interesting. I suppose I was inspired by the pie-in-the-face event and the dunk tank, both of which involved the teacher being humiliated. Students, I knew, liked that. That's when it came to me: boxing.

The way I saw it, students would pay pretty much anything to watch a pair of teachers—one of whom would be me—throwing punches at one another. I also knew who I could ask—I'd known the math teacher, one Rob Lundy, since Grade 8. We used to play hockey together. He was sporty. I was sporty. We were about the same height and weight. What could go wrong?

So I cornered him in the teachers' lunchroom.

"Rob," I said, "I've got an idea for ShareLife Day."

"Okay."

"Boxing. I get a ring in here and we fight. We'll get a referee, cornermen, you name it. You know. Make it look real."

"You want to fight me in front of the whole school?"

"Yes."

"Great," he said. "I'll do it."

We then went to the principal of De La Salle.

"Brother Domenic," I said, "Rob and I want to box for ShareLife Day. We'll get a ring in here, trainers, a referee. We'll charge everyone five dollars. Would you let us?"

"Yes," he said with a nod, "I would."

A week or two later, Rob went on a short ski trip with the students and dislocated his shoulder. So he was out. Fortunately, I had another candidate. That September, a teacher named Steve Mason had started at the school. He taught economics. He was also athletic and pretty much exactly my height and weight. I asked him if he'd be willing to box me. He shrugged. It was as though I'd asked him if he wanted to grab a coffee in the teachers' lounge.

"Sure," he said, "why not?"

Right away, I started looking into the world of boxing. After a couple of false starts, I reached a guy who ran a boxing club at Bloor and Yonge called Florida Jack's. We told Florida Jack what we wanted to do.

"Hmmm," he said. "Why dontcha come down to the club and we can talk about it?"

So Steve and I went. To reach it, you found a small door in an alley and walked up a flight of stairs into a classic old boxing club. A dozen punching bags hung from the ceiling. There were black-and-white photos of old boxers lining the stairwell. There were mirrors on one of the walls. There was a drink machine and weights and exercise equipment. There was also a regulation boxing ring with blue mats.

We asked to speak to Florida Jack. A minute later, a grizzled old guy walked out. He looked just like Burgess Meredith's character in *Rocky*.

"Whattya want?" he asked.

"I'm Gerry and this is Steve," I said. "We talked on the phone? About getting a ring set up in our high school for a day?"

"Oh, yeah. I remember. Who's gonna fight?"

I pointed toward Steve. "We are."

"And how long you want the fight to go?"

I looked at Steve. He looked at me.

"Well . . . fifteen rounds."

"Fifteen rounds?"

"We want it to look real."

"You'll die."

"What do you mean?"

"You can't do fifteen rounds. I'll let you do three."

We tried to convince him that fifteen rounds would be a better sell for the kids. He would have none of it. We agreed to three.

"Now," he said, "when you gonna start trainin'?"

Again, Steve and I looked at each other, confused.

"We weren't thinking we needed to train."

Florida Jack lifted an eyebrow. He pointed a crooked finger at each of us. "*You*," he said, "need to train."

"I don't think so," I said. "We both did university athletics. We're both in good shape. We both go on runs. I've even been in a hockey fight. So I don't think three rounds is going to a problem. Oh, and by the way, I'm going to phone a bunch of media. It'll be really good publicity for your club. I mean, if you agree to do it."

He looked wary. Though I couldn't imagine why, I could tell he wanted to say no. Yet I could also tell that he was enticed by the offer.

Finally, he took a deep breath and said, "Fine."

We didn't train. We didn't do anything. Actually, we did do one thing: we were both fitted with customized mouth-guards, but only because Florida Jack insisted.

The day before the fight, some guys from Florida Jack's showed up and set up the ring. Steve and I were excited. If it looked exactly like a real ring, it was because it *was* a real ring—there were ropes and buckles and a bright red bell and a bouncy floor. Plus, it smelled bad. I called the *Toronto Star*, the *Toronto Sun*, CityNews and 680 News and pitched them each a story about a pair of teachers at a Toronto Catholic school who were going to fight each other to raise money for ShareLife. One reporter asked if we thought this was a good idea.

"Do you have insurance?" he asked. "What if someone gets really hurt? How long have you both been boxing?"

Blah, blah, blah. We had thought none of this through, and we weren't too concerned. At the very least, Steve and I talked right before the fight, just to be safe. "Listen, we're not *really* going to fight, are we? We're just going to sort of make it look like we're fighting, right?"

"Totally," he said. "I mean, we both have to go back to work the next day."

"So, like, body shots only?"

"Body shots only," he said. "Nothing above the shoulders."

"Done."

This made me feel better. The fight was at noon. I knew nothing about Steve's fighting background, and mine pretty much didn't exist, unless you counted British bulldog at recess. Around eleven, Florida Jack showed up with two cornermen and a referee. He gave us boxing trunks, shoes and robes. We went off and got changed. Then he gave us headgear. He also gave us sixteen-ounce boxing gloves, which are the heaviest gloves you can use. "They punch a lot lighter," he explained. "This way, you might not kill each other."

We were standing in the hall outside the auditorium. I turned to Steve. "So, like we agreed, yeah? Punches to *this* area only." I then took one of those great, big boxing gloves and sort of indicated an area bordered by my waist and my shoulders.

"Right," Steve said. "'Course. Body shots only."

"No punches to the head."

"No punches to the head."

Florida Jack was beside us, chuckling. What, I wondered, did he know that we didn't?

I entered the gymnasium. I'd never seen it so full. Immediately, the kids started to boo me. I guess I'd given out too many detentions over the years. As I climbed into the ring, Steve entered. The place went nuts. He shadowboxed around the ring, playing it up for the audience. We took off our robes and stood in our corners. The referee was another old-timer—not as old as Florida Jack, but obviously a guy who'd been around boxing rings for the whole of his adult life.

It was just like in the movies. He wore black pants and a white shirt and his hair was slicked back, like they used to do in the '40s. His voice was booming.

"Ladies and gentlemen, in this corner, weighing in at five foot ten and 180 pounds, Mister Don-a-huuuuuugh!"

He waited for the booing to subside. I was surprised by how long this took.

"And in this corner, weighing in at five foot nine and 170 pounds, Mr. Maaaaaa-son."

There was cheering. Steve danced with his arms in the air.

We went to the centre of the ring. The referee put a hand on each of our shoulders and spoke quickly. "Gentlemen I want a good clean fight no blows below the belt always protect yourself now touch gloves if you want to and go to your corners."

We touched gloves. We went to our corners. I was officially nervous. The referee hit the bell and we came charging out of our corners.

Call it the law of the jungle, call it survivor's instinct, call it that stupid male desire to win at all costs: our gentlemen's agreement went away, and we started to try to kill each other. We were swinging for each other's heads. We were throwing uppercuts at the chin. We were throwing haymakers. Within fifteen seconds, my arms felt so heavy I could barely lift them. My shoulders were so full of lactic acid that they felt on fire. Thirty seconds in, we were in a clinch against the ropes, and I heard Steve say to me, "Gerry . . . I can't do this . . . I can't breathe . . . please don't hit me right now."

"Don't worry," I said. "I can't lift my arms."

We hung on. The bell rang. I went to my corner. I couldn't get my breath. I was so, so exhausted. The mouthguard didn't help; I asked my cornerman to take it out. He tried, but the mouthguard fit tightly, and as he tried to get it out of my mouth, it rubbed, hard, against my gum line. Now I was bleeding from the mouth. He gave up. I still couldn't catch my breath. He squirted water into my mouth, and I spat bloody water into a bucket. Had I a moment to think, I might have reflected on how absurd this all was—a friendly sporting match, to raise money for a worthy cause, and here I was, spitting blood in front of my students.

But there was no time to think. Did you know that the rest time between rounds in boxing is one minute? Did you know that, for the boxers, this passes in a nanosecond? The bell rang. I came out. We boxed. Steve clipped me. I cannot adequately describe the sensation of being punched in the head, except to say that the legs turn weak, you go dizzy, your vision goes weird and you feel like you want to throw up. And yet, it is not just those things, all put together. It's something more disorienting and awful— that's what people mean when they say, "It felt like I got punched in the head."

The ref parted us. He gave me a standing eight count. The room stopped revolving and I could see straight again. We went back at it. This time, I clipped Steve—not as hard as he'd hit me, but hard enough that he got a standing eight count. Meanwhile, my thumb had been hyperextended. I didn't know this was possible when the hand is secured by a boxing glove, but it is. If I had trained, I realized, someone might've shown me how to correctly throw a punch. But I hadn't, and now it felt as though I'd broken my thumb. We went back to the centre of the ring and started hitting each other again. Neither of us could breathe. We could barely stand. We both kept taking glimpses at the timekeeper, an art teacher named Mr. Lue Tam, as if to say, "Are you sure this round isn't over? That felt like *eight* minutes."

The bell sounded. I went back to my corner. I still couldn't breathe. I was still spitting blood. I cannot tell you how much I dreaded going back out there. Here is the thing about boxing: There are sports in which you become extremely, extremely tired. Squash comes to mind. Water polo is another. Yet in those sports, if you become too winded to play well, the only consequence is that you will play poorly. If it happens in boxing, it is highly probable that you will be hit in the face. That's what I'd learned after six whole minutes in a boxing ring. The consequences are far more severe than in any other sport.

The bell rang. We went out. We were still trying to kill each other. Yet it wasn't really fighting, since our legs could barely hold us up and we could barely keep our hands in the air and both of us wanted this thing to be over. Finally, the bell rang. We hugged, but we couldn't speak. Too tired. We stumbled back to our corners and sat. They called it a no-decision. I think that was fair. The punch Steve had landed in round two was the hardest of the day, and yet there were a couple of times I'd had him against the ropes and had backed up to let him out. So a draw was fine with me. I was too tired to care, anyway.

We raised seven hundred dollars that day. No! After paying Florida Jack and his team for everything, we *cleared* seven hundred. I'm pretty sure I preferred the pink eye from the dunk tank; on the other hand, we had created a moment that the school talks about to this day.

I couldn't straighten my thumb for a month. Steve told me he had trouble catching his breath for the rest of the week. We were both sore for months. And while I don't think boxing should be banned, I do think you should have some sort of certificate before you're allowed to box—some sort of licence that shows you've trained and know what you're doing. Or maybe a quick boxing course in teachers' college for idiots like us.

Am I glad I did it? Or was it just another of my impulsive, ill-conceived plans that I didn't think through? Yes and yes. I was glad I survived—that counts for something. Twenty-three years later, Steve Mason and I are still the best of friends. That counts for something as well. From that day on, I've had maximum respect for boxers. I honestly don't know how they do what they do. And for fifteen rounds! I learned I wasn't in great shape. I learned that if some grizzled old boxing club owner tells you that you need to learn how to do something before you do it, you should listen. I also learned how heavy your own head becomes when you are truly, truly exhausted. Honestly—it weighs a ton. But mostly, it gave me a good story. If ever I'm out somewhere and the subject of difficult sports comes up, I just let the others talk. Then, when there's a break in the conversation, I deal the ace up my sleeve.

"By any chance," I say, "have any of you ever boxed?"

# THE BEST EDUCATION
# I EVER HAD

Education is a fairly structured system, one that is set up pretty much the same way all around the world. While some countries move at a different pace, they all follow a curriculum that directs students toward a higher education—at least, that's the hope. Along the way, you learn many things. You take many subjects, whether you like them or not. Families put a lot of trust in this system, and for the most part, it works quite well. I, for one, learned many things at school, but mostly because I was forced to learn them. I learned how clouds work during precipitation, and I learned how to solve the third side of a right-angled triangle when I only know the lengths of the other two sides. I can honestly say I would have survived quite well in life had I not known these two things. I've never once had to recall this information, except when teaching it to my kids. In fact, most of the things

I've learned in life that have gotten me where I am now are things I learned in a different form of education: working.

I had my first job at the age of ten. That's right, ten. Like many people of my generation, I had a paper route. Now, keep in mind, I had to have a paper route if I wanted to have any money as a kid. Don't get me wrong, my parents supplied me with all the basics in life. They also looked after my hockey, baseball and golf needs. They did all of this, however, on a pretty strict budget. If I wanted to do anything extra, or have some money for myself, I had to work. In the 1980s, delivering papers was a typical job for kids at younger ages, but perhaps not the safest. One year, I delivered the *Globe and Mail*, which had to be on people's doorsteps by 7 a.m. This meant a 6 a.m. wakeup call from my father or mother to prepare the papers and be on my way. It was a lonely, dark walk—I'm surprised my father, who worried as much as he did, would let me walk my street alone in the pre-dawn pitch dark. I never thought twice about it, and obviously, neither did he. I often think of how easy it would have been to kidnap me. Ten years old, four foot two, sixty pounds with a satchel full of newspapers. I could have fit in the satchel, making it even easier to take me. Ironically, the news of the kidnapping would have been in the newspaper. Perhaps the world was safer back then; today, I would never let my ten-year-old son do such a thing, especially for the measly fifty dollars a week I was making. The responsibility I took on was a lot for a ten-year-old, but the money I received at the end of each week made it all worthwhile.

Eventually, I switched from delivering the *Globe and Mail* to the *Toronto Star*, which came out in the afternoon back then, so it was delivered after school. This, at least, allowed me to do my route in daylight, when other humans were walking around. But it also meant missing out on anything that happened after school. Again, it was the sort of responsibility that prepared me for life, something that the Pythagorean theorem never did.

At seventeen, I took a job at a Dominion supermarket, where I stocked shelves, mopped floors and did price checks. This was also the first time I had bosses. They were like teachers, in some ways, but they could fire me if I wasn't doing my job. (Sometimes I wonder if the school system would work better if we could fire bad students.) It was also the first time I was put into a customer service role. The way you talked to customers and dealt with them was important. Do a good job of it, and you stay. Do a bad job, and you get fired. It's really how society should work, and for the most part, it *is* how it works. Except for school. They rarely fail kids anymore, and good luck trying to kick a bad student out of school. It's almost impossible in the public school system.

By eighteen, I took the job that would mould my life in so many ways: I became a waiter at The Keg. Nothing prepared me more for life than my ten years working there. Let's start with their training program. In the words of Drake, you started at the bottom. Regardless of how old you were, who you knew or how much experience you might have had in the industry, you started in the dish pit. And let me tell you, there is nothing fun about working in the dish pit at a restaurant. You did this for two weeks, and then you worked the salad bar, then on to the line, cooking meals, and eventually you started busing tables. After that, you'd be placed at the hosting stand, where you were the first person to greet customers as they arrived at the restaurant. If this all went well and you stuck it out, you would eventually train as a server—or bartender, if you were the right age.

This experience taught me so much about respecting others and their positions in the restaurant. There were full-time dishwashers and full-time bussers. There were full-time hosts and hostesses, and there were full-time cooks who worked for six to eight hours every night in the confines of a heat-filled kitchen. The servers and bartenders made the most money, so theirs were often the most sought-after positions. They also got all the credit by way of tips. Yet The Keg's training program taught you that it was a team effort, and that you should never think you were above anyone else. Having to spend a few weeks as a dishwasher prevented you from thinking you were better than the people doing that job, because you knew how tough and boring it was. You learned to be aware of the staff who might not be getting all the accolades and money. Most of all, it taught you how to work with, and appreciate, people from every background and every walk of life.

Waiting tables taught me so much about communication, teamwork and money. Yes, money—how to make it, and how to lose it. You did a bad job, and your tips reflected it. I also learned about time management and multi-tasking. On any given night, you were responsible for six to eight tables, all of which were at different points in the service: one table had just been seated, one was on dessert, one wanted more coffee, one wanted the bill and one needed their food. Managing this at the age of eighteen or nineteen was a handful—at *any* age, it was a fast-paced, pressure-filled six hours every night. And, if you did a bad job, you basically did it all for no money.

Legend has it that the word *tips* comes from an acronym standing for "To Insure Proper Service." Wherever it came from, tips were the lifeblood of any waiter or bartender.

Mentally, the job was very draining. At night, you'd get nightmares—we called them "Kegmares"—about all the things that could go wrong. They were horrible. So we learned to manage the stress of the job on top of all the other pieces of life education we were soaking up. Again, not once did I apply anything I learned in school about cumulus or stratus clouds.

And the lying! You have to do it. Being honest often meant no tips. "Where is my food?" was a common question from tables. The standard answer was always "The kitchen is really backed up, but I've asked them to move your order forward." The kitchen wasn't backed up; I just forgot to ring in the order. I hated getting tea for customers because it involved a lot of items: a cup, a tea bag, a spoon, a little pot with hot water, some milk, some sugar and a side plate. That's a lot of time and a lot of running around for something that I might make twenty cents on. So, I'd do what was easier: I'd tell people we were out of tea.

I would never have gotten into stand-up comedy if I hadn't worked at The Keg. The restaurant industry is filled with staff who are aspiring comedians and actors who are working nights so as to keep their days free for auditions. Being immersed in this group was a great push for me to enter the industry. In some ways, we performed every single night for our tables. At least, at The Keg, we did. Their motto was to "wow" the guests. Now, don't get me wrong, serving quality food in a timely manner was the most important aspect of the job. But on top of that, if you could "wow" your guests, you would take their experience to another level. I would "wow" them with comedy. Or, at least, I'd try to.

I guess you could say my stand-up career started at The Keg, long before I ever stepped onto a real stage. Most of the time, my audience was small—maybe two to four people—but once in a while I would get a large party of twenty, and I loved that. The bigger the crowd, the better it is for a comedian. I would rip on anything I could with the table—their outfits, their boss, anything to make them laugh.

Sometimes it would backfire because I'd spend too much time with a table where I was "killing it," which would mean other tables would suffer by getting poor service. So, I'd have to work hard to try to win those tables back. Much later, I'd do the same thing in stand-up whenever I sensed I was losing a crowd. Sometimes it worked, but if it didn't, it cost me money. Again, this was a life lesson I couldn't learn at school.

Working at The Keg also taught me a lot about math; you get very sharp at working out percentages, so you can tell what a good tip is, and what a bad tip is.

Eventually, when my stand-up comedy began to take off, I left The Keg. But about three years into my career as a comedian, I received an offer to do a gig for a small company that had booked its Christmas party at a restaurant. That was very common. The thing is, they didn't book a private room or anything like that; they simply reserved a table for twenty in the main part of the restaurant. When I arrived at the gig, I realized very quickly that I would be performing my act, with no microphone, at the end of the table. While it was very strange—the other tables were right beside us—it was something I was very comfortable with. It felt like I was back in my waitering days, except the pay was a lot better.

Going to school is a must for any child, but nothing prepares them for the real world like a job. I would even go a step further and suggest a job in the restaurant business. I can't tell you how many friends I still have from those days working at The Keg, and I still pop in and see some of the staff who worked there when I did. When I'm on the road, I still visit Keg locations—once a Kegger, always a Kegger. It was the best education I ever had. So, while I may not be able to tell you the atomic mass of a certain element from the periodic table, I can tell you which steaks go best with certain wines. It's the same thing, really.

Oh, and one more thing: decaffeinated coffee isn't always made, so when you order it from a waiter, please be forewarned that you may end up being served regular coffee. Just a heads-up.

# PART FOUR

**Family and Other Headaches**

# PUNY

I was born at exactly 11:45 p.m. on December 31, 1968. This meant that, every year, I was by far the youngest kid in my class. Had I been born just fifteen minutes later, I would have been the oldest. This would have helped.

I really was huge—I weighed in at a hefty nine pounds, seven ounces. I was also among the one in two thousand children who are born with a pair of immense front teeth—they're called natal teeth, apparently. Though I never asked my mum, I assume I was bottle-fed.

So, I started the world big. I just didn't grow as quickly as other children. By the time I reached kindergarten, I was sort of average size. But with each passing year, I got smaller and smaller relative to the other kids. By Grade 2, I was among the smallest half of the class. By Grade 3, I was among the smallest third. By Grade 4, I was among the smallest quarter. At times, it almost felt like I was shrinking.

And yet, I had this compulsion to run the schoolyard. When it came time to pick teams, I always had to be one of the captains. And as I've said, I was also super competitive and absolutely hated to lose. Playing road hockey, I'd literally throw myself into my bodychecks. It's just the way I was: I wanted to win, at all costs.

And you may well ask: How on earth did I get away with this, given that, with each passing year, I got smaller, and smaller, and smaller? It's simple. I was really good at sports, one of the best in my grade at St. Gabriel Catholic School. This helped. Yet I also had a secret weapon, an ace up my sleeve: my brother. His name was Kevin, and he was the toughest kid in the neighbourhood. Kevin would fight anyone, at any time, and it didn't matter if that person was older, or stronger, or had a buddy with him: when it was time for Kevin to fight, he fought. I remember my father telling me about the time he first realized that Kevin was going to be a fighter.

"This was back in Glasgow," he told me. "I was at home, looking out the window, when I happened to see this older kid bothering your sister. Your brother was there. He calmly rolled up his sleeves and punched the other kid in the face. And he was all of five years old, Gerry! All of five years old!"

Once, I asked my brother how many fights he'd had in his life.

"You mean, how many hockey fights?"

"All fights. Hockey fights, schoolyard fights, bar fights, you know, all of them."

"Hmm," he said, stroking his chin. "Maybe two hundred?"

"And how many times did you lose?"

"None. I tied a kid once in Grade 8. But I never lost."

He was five years older than me. He went to the same school as me. If anyone ever laid a hand on me, I didn't have to tell him; he'd just know about it. He had an interesting way of distributing justice. He wouldn't beat up the kid who'd picked on me. No, that would've made him look like a bully. Instead, he'd find out if the kid who'd picked on me had an older brother, and he'd get a message to him. This amounted to an effective form of peacekeeping. The older kids would tell the other kids, "Don't you touch Kevin Donoghue's brother." And so they never did. This went on for years.

Years later, when I was at York, I once went to a new bar that had opened up near campus. I was dancing away when some guy came up from behind me, reached around and smashed me in the face with a beer bottle. The top of the bottle hit me high on the cheekbone. I fell. The guy's buddy stepped on my face. People started screaming, and the two ran away. I don't remember any of it because I had been knocked out cold.

I awoke in my room on campus. Two of my friends had walked me back. When I told my brother Kevin on the phone, he said he was coming to "fix" it, even though he was seven hours away, attending Western Michigan University on a hockey scholarship.

"What happened?" he asked.

"Two guys jumped me at the school pub."

"Why?"

"I have no idea."

"Did you know them?"

"No."

"Could you recognize them?"

"My friend Ilir could."

"We're going back there."

"Kevin, they're long gone."

"Of course they're gone. But I know one thing: they're gonna come back."

He insisted that he come. I told him I was fine and we had no idea who these guys were, so he agreed not to bother. That's how he was. Very protective. He still is. He's almost sixty years old. He'd fight anyone, especially if it was to protect someone in his family. He's the toughest guy I ever met.

I continued to get smaller, relative to my schoolmates. I remember my parents telling me not to worry, that there were no short people in my family, and that one day, when my body was good and ready, I would grow. I also remember our family doctor telling me that I had long bones, whatever that means, and that I would one day grow to a height that, at the very least, approached the middle of the bell curve. This was small consolation. By Grade 7, I was four feet, ten inches tall. I weighed seventy pounds.

Meanwhile, there were two other guys who decided that they wanted to run the schoolyard. Sean was five foot seven and weighed about 150 pounds. His first lieutenant was named Mike; he was just as tall as Sean, and just as heavy. Sean wasn't a fan of mine. Although he never said why, I assumed it was because this small kid, who was good at sports, was also too chirpy for his own good. So he resented me and felt threatened by me. Given that he was literally twice my size, it would've been as easy to beat me to a pulp as cross the street on a green light. Yet there was my secret weapon: even though my brother had left the school, we all lived in the same neighbourhood, and they all knew him. Sean, meanwhile, had an older brother who, quite rightly, feared my brother. Now, don't get me wrong, I was no cup of tea to deal with in grade school, either. Bossy, competitive and chirpy. *So* chirpy. I was very confident in who I was. Small and confident is not always a good combination. These guys just played mental games with me, and I'm sure I did the same to some of them when we were younger. What goes around comes around, and it was coming around in droves.

They resorted mostly to psychological torture and exclusion. Exclusion for a kid is almost worse. They'd try to tease me about my size and my enormous front teeth, though they would learn quickly that you can't heckle a heckler. Where it got tough was when we played sports or British bulldog and they would try to kill me. "Try to catch me," I would say. I was also fast. Not the fastest, but faster than Sean and Mike. So, their frustration was building. They would try to bodycheck me in hockey or soccer, but I was way better than all of them at both sports. At the time, we played a schoolyard sport that we called foot hockey. Basically, it was tennis-ball hockey, but instead of a stick, you used your feet. I loved playing foot hockey, and they knew it. I'd show up to school, and if the kids were already playing, Sean would tell me there was no more space on the teams. Soon, word started to spread: Sean was taking over. You could either pick him, or stick with the old leader, Gerry Donoghue.

So I ask: Who would you have picked? There were girls in Grade 3 who looked older than me. Sean, with a small adjustment in his mannerisms, could have gotten served at a bar. Suddenly, I was alone, sidelined, outplayed, out-gunned. The fact that I couldn't do anything about it—that I couldn't march up to Sean and tell him we should have it out, right here, right now, no holds barred, just you and me—made me feel smaller still.

Things got worse. At the time, when I was on any sports field, I had a habit of adjusting myself: my shorts, my pants, my belt, whatever. It's a nervous tic employed by baseball players, and I'd somehow picked it up for myself. One day, I got to school, hoping to play a little foot hockey. From a distance, I could see that Sean was pacing around the track with all of his henchmen: Mike, Nick, John, James, Joe, the list went on and on. They were locking arms and chanting something. As I got closer, I could faintly hear what they were chanting: it had something to do with me. I got a little closer, and a little closer, until finally I could hear what they were chanting: "Gerry picks his balls!"

I had one friend named Alan. Alan was with me through all of this. Sure, I had lots of fake friends who were nice to me when Sean and Mike weren't gathering them to chant "Gerry picks his balls." But Alan, he was loyal and a true friend. I never, ever forgot that, and it must have been hard for him. He could either jump in with the masses, like Nick and Steve and Joe did, or remain loyal and hang out with me. What a great guy! He walked with me while the song continued in the background.

It was the most humiliating thing that had ever happened to me. What really hurt was that there were a lot of girls hanging around, and by Grade 7 I had started to like girls. In fact, at the time, I had a girlfriend named Tiffany. Ours was the most innocent relationship imaginable. We never kissed, not even once, over two years. In fact, the sum total of our romantic relationship occurred at a matinee screening at the Bayview Village Cinemas. We went on a double date with Steve and another girl in our class named Bobbi. Halfway through the movie, I put an arm around Tiffany, finally making my first move since we'd been "going around," as we called it, for almost two years. Come Monday, Bobbi told everybody that I "tried to make out with Tiffany in the movie theatre." What? So now, according to the female population of St. Gabriel's Catholic School, I was guilty of two major offences:

1. I got handsy in movie theatres.
2. I picked my balls.

Looking back, I almost have to admire the deviousness of Sean and his crew. They'd destroyed me without laying a finger on me. It would have been better if he'd simply beaten me up. At least I might have received some sympathy. How

I longed to put Sean in his place, using the only language he understood.

So I went to my brother and told him I wanted to learn how to fight.

"Okay," was his answer.

We put on gym clothes and sneakers and went to the soccer field at Elkhorn Public School, which was across the street. We jogged around the park to warm up. Then we stretched, did a few jumping jacks and shadow boxed. Kevin had brought along two pairs of boxing gloves and some kick pads. Yes, he owned these. We put everything on. I still remember the feeling of power I had when I slipped my tiny hands into the boxing gloves. Then he looked at me. We were standing about five feet apart.

"Come at me," he said.

I blinked. "What do you mean?"

"I want you to come at me with everything you got. Kick me, punch me, whatever you can think of to attack me."

Suddenly, I felt nervous. "I . . . I don't want to come at you."

"You want me to teach you to fight?"

"Yeah."

"Then come at me. With everything you've got."

I screamed, charged and tried to punch him on the nose. Before I could touch him, he gave me a hard roundhouse kick to the stomach. I grabbed my midsection and fell to the turf. I couldn't breathe. For the next minute or so, I really felt as though I was about to suffocate. He helped me up. Pain was radiating from my stomach. Every part of me hurt.

I remember looking at him through damp eyes. And that was it. The fight training was over after about twenty-five seconds. We packed up our stuff and headed back home. He felt terrible that he hit me. "I thought you knew something about fighting. Even just an instinct to block my foot."

No. I knew nothing. I felt like saying, "That's why we were there, dumbass."

I developed a plan B: I'd noticed that if I got to school early, when only one or two of Sean's "gang" were there, they wouldn't torment me (or, at least, they wouldn't torment me as badly). I'm still not sure why this was, exactly, though there did seem to be a belief, deeply held among schoolyard bullies, that planning what to do to their victim wasn't as fun if the victim was standing right there. So I got to school early. I stopped eating breakfast. I made excuses to my parents: "I've got soccer practice early." It was the same at recess and lunch. As soon as the bell rang, I'd throw myself out of my seat and race for the door. I did this all through Grade 7. By the time I got to Grade 8, I didn't even realize I was doing it.

In the Toronto Catholic school system, you could apply to only three of the Catholic high schools. It was assumed that I would go to an all-boys school—I don't even think we had any coed Catholic high schools in my area back then. To be honest, I wasn't on the radar of any of the girls, so I was fine with this. Since I lived within three miles of Brebeuf College School, my parents naturally assumed I'd go there. There was one problem: Sean and his boys were going there. If I didn't want to spend another five years (remember, we went to Grade 13 back then) listening to them chant "Gerry picks his balls" whenever I wasn't the first guy to school. I'd have to go elsewhere. Besides, most of my friends from hockey outside of school were going to St. Michael's College School. So I submitted my choices as St. Michael's College, De La Salle and Brebeuf—the last one only because you needed to name three. But I had no doubt I would get into St. Mike's. For the next few months, whenever people asked me where I'd be going for high school, my answer was always very confident: "I'm going to St. Mike's."

I wasn't accepted. Apparently, I lived outside their boundaries. My parents and I tried everything to change their minds. No luck. Friends I played hockey with, who lived a few blocks away, got in; I guess they were just inside this boundary. Heartbroken, I sat down with my parents in the living room and said I wanted to go to De La Salle. Though I knew very little about the school, my sister spoke highly of it because she'd performed in a lot of musicals there. Regardless of what I did or didn't know, there was no way I was going to Brebeuf to face the world of Sean, Mike, Joe, James, Nick, Stephen and John.

"Don't be ridiculous," my dad insisted. "Brebeuf is right down the street. Why would you go all the way down to De La Salle when you don't know anyone?"

"I'll tell you why," I said, through tears.

For the first time, I explained everything to my parents. Everything about how miserable these guys made my life. They were shocked and saddened to learn that I had kept all

214

of this in for the past two years. My mum gave me a big hug and my dad agreed right away. "De La Salle it is!"

So, off I went to De La Salle in downtown Toronto. It was far. I would walk fifteen minutes to catch the Sheppard bus to Yonge Street, where I would hop onto the subway for another twenty minutes to St. Clair station, before walking another fifteen minutes to campus. (Actually, I'd run the last fifteen, as I was usually late.)

I was excited for the students at De La Salle to meet me. After all, I'd been the best athlete at St. Gabriel's, where I'd been light years ahead of everyone in hockey, baseball, soccer, football, tennis and golf. As I started Grade 9, I still looked like the average Grade 6 kid. But what they didn't know was that I was an athletic weapon, and I was eager for them to find out.

How wrong I was. De La Salle was full of athletes. Tons of them. I would either get cut from teams or, if I made them, I would hardly play. And forget about making the junior hockey team, the football team or the soccer team. I wasn't even good enough to try out. I managed to make the bantam hockey team, which was for the players who couldn't make the junior team. I also played tennis and golf, which very few kids did. So, now I was still small, still chirpy and a middle-of-the-pack athlete. I was humbled, to say the least.

The top dog in Grade 9, meanwhile, was a guy named Greg O'Halloran, who clocked in at six foot two. He, like Sean, ran the grade. But the difference was that Greg was a great athlete and didn't exclude you. In fact, he was the opposite: if you were good at something, he appreciated you. He was also very secure in who he was. He did like to tease me, but at the same time, if anyone touched me, he would be the first person to stick up for me. I think he was amused by this little guy who wouldn't back down in sports. At the same time, he wouldn't take any of my chirping. In fact, one day he threw me in a locker for thirty seconds to teach me a lesson. It didn't matter; we fast became close friends anyway.

I grew six inches in the summer between Grades 10 and 11. Suddenly, I was five foot six. Even better, my giant front teeth were now proportional, more or less, to the rest of my body.

The problem now was my weight. I was stuck at 115 pounds. I remember one day, I took off my shirt in gym class and some guy said, "Jesus, are you okay? Your ribs are sticking out." It was probably Greg who said it, but I can't remember.

No matter what I did, I couldn't gain weight. By all rights, I should have; I had the worst diet imaginable. I ate cookies for breakfast. For lunch, I always had the same thing: two hash browns, fries with gravy, chocolate milk and potato chips. I'd drink cans of Pepsi, though in a strange way. For a while, instead of a pull tab, cans of Pepsi had two small holes—one big one and one small one. Instead of popping them both, I'd open the big one, hold the can to my mouth and squeeze, jetting the syrupy liquid into my mouth. With all that sugar in my system, I was hyperactive. I never stopped moving. I went everywhere with a hockey bag over my shoulder. Plus, I was growing. This takes a lot of calories as well.

By York University, I reached my full height: five feet, ten inches tall. Still only 135 pounds. Once I stopped growing, I started putting on weight: by the start of my teacher's degree at St. Francis Xavier, I was clocking in at 155. This figure has ticked up as I've aged: recently, I was shocked to realize that I needed to lose some weight for a role I was taking. Yes, that's right: according to science, I am now slightly obese.

Today, my son is small. In Grade 5, he's under four and a half feet tall and weighs all of sixty pounds. Yet he's not going through what I went through. He's not mouthy like I was, and doesn't attract unwanted rivalries. There's also a lot of anti-bullying instruction in schools, which I'm thankful for. I've also told him not to worry, that one day, just like I did, he'll start to grow. Sooner than later, I imagine he'll be taller than I am. He'll get bigger and I'll get smaller. In fact, it's already started to happen: the other day, my doctor told me that I was now five foot nine and three-quarters.

After all these years, it turns out I really am shrinking.

# BRYLCREEM ON THE TOOTHBRUSH

My parents met at a policemen's ball in 1955. My father, a policeman, was twenty-two. He'd recently broken his arm while chasing a criminal and was wearing a cast. My mother was nineteen years old and was still living with her parents. She was young and pretty. My father looked handsome in his uniform. Without so much as opening his mouth, he came across as honest and hard-working—it had something to do with the way he held himself. I'm sure they found a lot of common interests as they chatted that night, but what mattered most to both of them, and their parents, was that they were both Catholic.

That was a huge deal back then; it would be unheard of for either of them to date, let alone marry, a Protestant. At that time, in Glasgow, religion played a big role in determining which school you went to, where you lived, who you dated and, of course, which football (soccer) team you supported. So, Catholics marrying Catholics was all that was accepted. Those who deviated from that unwritten rule paid the price in their families and communities.

The ball was held at the Bundoran Club, on Sauchiehall Street, which happened to be one of Glasgow's best-known streets. My father always told me that when you entered the Bundoran, you knew that everyone in there was Catholic, since they had to recite the Confiteor before entering. Imagine, standing at the door, reciting the following to the doorman:

> *I confess to Almighty God, to blessed Mary, ever Virgin,*
> *to blessed Michael the Archangel,*
> *to blessed John the Baptist,*
> *to the holy Apostles Peter and Paul,*
> *to all the Saints and to you, Father,*
> *that I have sinned exceedingly, in thought, word and deed,*
> *through my fault, through my fault, through my most*
> *grievous fault . . .*

. . . and so on.

My parents dated for five years and married in 1960. By then, Dad was twenty-seven, Mum was twenty-four. My sister, Angela, was born in 1961. My brother, Kevin, was born in 1963. It was a time when their friends and family were leaving for Canada and America. My father's plan was America—the land of opportunity, as they said. So, he started the process. He had a connection for a job from another police officer in the US. He filed his immigration paperwork but had missed a section of his application. They sent it back to him, along with an explanation as to what was missing. During this process, which was going to take months, my mother's older brother Jimmy, who had already immigrated to Canada, came back home to Scotland for a visit. He raved about Canada and convinced my father and mother to move there. And so, they did. In October of 1965, my dad set sail alone on the RMS *Carinthia*, just one of almost nine hundred passengers. (He hated the idea of flying and always said if anything happened on a boat, he could swim a hundred feet, but he couldn't fly an inch.) Six months later, my mother, sister and brother followed by plane. Any money they had saved was spent on travel, and they landed, like many immigrants, completely broke.

Living in a new country is hard. Living with no money is even harder, but being away from his wife and young kids was perhaps the hardest for my dad during that first six months. I remember him telling me stories over the years about how hard it was. What made his first few weeks even worse was that, about two weeks before he left, he took a big chunk of the money he'd saved and entered a poker game, where, predictably, he lost everything. As he would later tell me: "I wanted to try and get some more money before I left. I took a chance and I lost. It was a big mistake."

His first order of business was to apply to become a policeman. He thought this would be a no-brainer after thirteen years of service with the Glasgow police. He had an amazing letter of recommendation from his superiors. He was also young, fit and ready to serve and protect in

Canada. To his surprise, that was not to be the case. He was rejected. He couldn't understand why. It wasn't until years later, as he was reading a book on the life of former Toronto police chief Bill McCormack, that he realized it might have been because he was Catholic. At least that's what Bill said in his book—that when *he* applied, it was difficult to get on the force in Toronto if you were Catholic. The difference is that Bill figured it out and fought the system. My dad did not. So now he had to find a job and he had to find one fast.

My uncle Jimmy had offered my father a place to stay while he got settled. Well, a couch, really. But my father soon realized that Jimmy and his wife weren't keen on him staying too long. He actually overheard them discussing how inconvenient it was becoming; nobody likes a brother-in-law sleeping on their sofa for too long. Dad was fortunate to get a job fairly quickly, through another Scottish connection, at the de Havilland aircraft company. This would allow him to rent a room in the west end of Toronto and send most of his earnings back home to Scotland for my mother and siblings.

On his first day on the job, Dad had no money to get to work. No car. No bus fare. Nothing. He needed to take three buses; as he boarded each bus, he told the driver he had no money, but if they took his name and address, he'd send it in later. This was common practice in Scotland, apparently. In typical Canadian fashion, they all just told him to take a seat and not to worry about it. He did this for weeks until he got his first paycheque. And a co-worker, a fellow Scot, spotted him a few dollars until his first cheque arrived. This colleague was a big Celtic supporter and knew who my grandfather was from his days playing for Glasgow Celtic Football Club. It was a small world indeed.

Dad hated the job. He spent his whole day counting nuts and bolts for the planes. Life sucked for him. I don't imagine it was a picnic for my mother, either. But they did what they had to do.

As he got more settled, and grew to despise his job more and more, he saw an ad for a job at the Simpsons department store downtown. He jumped at it. Anything to get out of counting nuts and bolts. He would work in the toy section, which did little more than remind him of the two kids he had back in Scotland. At Simpsons, he met one of his best friends, Bill Wallace. That's right, his best friend had the same name as the famous Scottish knight, William Wallace. My dad's best friend was Protestant. They probably wouldn't have connected had they met back in Scotland because of the general segregation of the two religions. But in Canada, it was the birth of an amazing friendship. They would play snooker together, golf together and just hang out together.

My dad always said that Bill's positivity helped my dad through many tough days. Bill kept my dad's spirits up. He made him laugh and spent a lot of time with him. Sadly, Bill would die in his forties from cancer. To this day, Dad still talks about his first and closest Canadian friend. Without Bill, I don't think my dad would have lasted in Canada. I guess you could say he was my father's Scottish knight.

The Simpsons job gave Dad a bit more security, but he was still barely surviving in his new country. At this point, he would've done anything to make more money. He would have worked overtime, would have done side jobs if he could get them, but the one thing he wouldn't do was commit fraud. There was a shady guy who worked at Simpsons who seemed to be doing quite well. He'd always bring my father coffee and spot him a few bucks to help him make ends meet. One day, he explained to my father that he didn't need the Simpsons job and that he only kept it to avoid suspicion.

"Suspicion of what?" my father asked.

It turned out that he had a side hustle involving some sort of workmen's compensation fraud. He offered to cut my dad in, saying he had about forty other guys helping run the scam. "Everyone's doing it, John," he told my father.

My dad refused. He didn't give it a second thought. As the guy tried to give him some comfortable explanation, my father knew it was all bad and all wrong. As much as this money would have changed his life considerably, it wasn't who my father was. He was poor in many regards, but rich with honesty. He pulled away from this man immediately, knowing they were not cut from the same cloth. A few months later, my dad found the man on the cover of a Toronto newspaper; he'd been arrested and charged with fraud. Everyone involved in the scam was brought down with him.

My father, his head held high, left Simpsons when he saw another opportunity open up at Standard Life, selling life insurance. This job, he did like. He was good at it. His honesty disarmed people and persuaded customers to believe in what he was selling. Plus, he got to travel. I have a picture of him from this time. He's standing in front of the Banff Springs Hotel, on the road with a bunch of other insurance salesmen, looking proud and healthy and so, so young.

One day, Dad had to attend a training session at the Toronto office. His boss gave a presentation, and at the end of the session, asked his team what they all thought of the presentation. No one spoke.

"Now, come on," he said. "Don't be shy."

"No need," one of the salesmen said. "It was really good."

"Top-notch," said another.

"Nothing to improve," said a third.

But my father? He looked at his boss and said, "Well, if you're asking me, I have to be honest. It was a little on the boring side. Is there anything you could do to make it a wee bit more interesting?"

A week later, Dad was let go. His boss said he had to cut back. Dad, however, knew better. "I should never have said that," he told me years later. And yet, he just couldn't help himself. That was my dad. It was as though he believed that God really would strike him down if he didn't tell the entire truth, all the time, under any circumstance.

On the upside, he soon found a job driving a bus for the Toronto Transit Commission (TTC). It offered good pay, lots of hours and a great pension. He seemed settled. It was a far cry from being a police officer, as he'd intended, but it was a secure job.

My father stayed at the TTC for the next twenty-three years. He detested every minute of every day on that job. The work was dull, he was harassed by riders, and the hours were terrible. He had to work a split shift. Up at three in the morning, he'd be behind the wheel at five. He'd drive until 9 a.m., go home, nap, and drive again from two until six. One morning, he told me, he was so tired that he accidentally brushed his teeth with Brylcreem.

For my eleventh birthday, he agreed to buy me a bicycle. I wanted the same one that all the kids at school seemed to have, a fancy two-hundred-dollar model from a local bike shop. He was willing to get me a sixty-dollar bike from Kmart. I made the mistake of complaining about it in front of a Kmart employee. Dad turned beet red and yelled, "Do you know how many times I had to drive up and down Finch Avenue to get you this bike?"

I don't know if there is a louder accent than Scottish when someone is yelling. The whole store could hear him, and I understand why. I had no idea what my mum and dad went through each day to provide financially for us. A two-hundred-dollar bike would be more than a week's salary for my father. It was a day that made me realize how hard they had it.

When I was a boy, he only ever hit me once. There was this really bad kid in the neighbourhood, who I'll call Jimmy G, who also went to my school. I wasn't allowed to play with him under any circumstances. I couldn't help but disobey my dad. Jimmy G was a good hockey goalie, and goalies were hard to find. He also owned a net, so we met near the mall and I took shots on him. We didn't do anything else. When I arrived back home, my father asked where I had been all day. I told him, "I was at Sean's house."

"Just Sean's house?"

"Yeah, well, we went to the mall for a bit."

"Oh," was his only reply.

Then he smacked me across the back of the head. A few times. He was less mad that I was playing with Jimmy G than he was that I lied. In fact, he was *only* mad that I had lied. He had driven by the mall and seen us playing together. Parents really do have eyes in the backs of their heads. Lesson learned.

# WHEN THE SAINTS GO MARCHING IN

**W**hile my dad was still at Standard Life, my mother, brother and sister came over in May 1966. By the spring of 1968, my mother was pregnant again.

On December 31, 1968, at 11:45 p.m., I was born. I was fifteen minutes away from being in the running to be the first baby born in Canada in 1969. Imagine, fifteen minutes away from fifteen minutes of fame on the day I was born. I always joked with my mum, "Could you not have held me in for fifteen more minutes?"

"You were huge. I wasn't holding you in for another second!"

She wasn't kidding. I was very late. I don't think inducing labour was a thing back then, but I was told that I was born weeks after my due date. My mum was close to losing me. In fact, she made a deal with St. Gerard Majella, the patron saint of expecting mothers. She prayed to him constantly, promising that if I was born healthy, she'd name me after him.

Voila. The birth of Gerard Francis Donoghue.

We were living in Scarborough, in a small two-bedroom apartment on Sheppard Avenue East. When my dad was on his own, he had been able to rent a bedroom in someone else's apartment. He didn't need much space, and it was all he could afford. When Mum, Angela and Kevin moved over from Scotland, and I was born, we needed more space and, as a result, more money. Losing his job at Standard Life couldn't have come at a worse time.

Things started to get really tough for Mum and Dad. I'm sure it was no picnic for Angela and Kevin, either. I guess my parents decided this was too much for all of them. Mum was stuck in a small apartment with three kids, while Dad was ready to give up. In the end, they decided that Mum would head back to Scotland with the kids, and Dad would try a little longer to find work, at which point he'd bring everyone back to Canada. Either that, or they'd forget the whole thing and settle back in their homeland. In his mind, it was over, but for some reason, he wanted to give Canada one more chance.

I never understood that. He had no family here, no job and no money. He had very few friends, but something told him Canada was worth fighting for. He was ready to give it one more try. He always told me that he thought there was more to do here in Canada. So, he borrowed some money from one of his friends at Standard Life, Ed Walker, and sent us all back to Scotland.

I was about two years old, so I don't remember any of this. My mother had a friend named Maggie Cullen who looked after a house that was owned by the local priest. It was a big house, and she arranged for my mum, brother and sister and me to live there until Dad either got settled and brought us back over, or he gave up and moved back to Scotland. I think they all expected the latter.

The priest had a German shepherd. One day, my brother was upstairs with Maggie and the dog when the dog attacked him. My sister, who was about ten, heard lots of screaming and panic. Maggie then came downstairs, carrying Kevin, who was covered in blood. The dog had tried to rip his arm off and would have been successful had Maggie not saved him. Kevin was about seven or eight years old at the time.

He was rushed to hospital, where he needed fifty stitches to sew up his arm. What a traumatic experience for him. He is the toughest person I know, yet to this day, he still shies away from big dogs whenever he sees them.

I can't imagine my dad hearing this news back in Canada, and the sense of helplessness of not being there to help his young son.

When my mum, siblings and I returned to Canada when I was five, we all moved into an apartment in Willowdale. It was in a homely three-storey building at 688 Sheppard Avenue East. When I turned eight, we moved to a townhouse at 11 Elkhorn Drive. It was a lot nicer than the apartment on Sheppard. It even had a little backyard. And when I say little, I mean little. It was about twenty feet by twenty feet. But it was home for us, and my parents had come a long way to get to this point. Mum had been working as a dental assistant, and Dad was working lots of overtime at the TTC, which paid him time and a half. Both of them hated their jobs and they still lived from paycheque to paycheque.

Still, we seemed to be doing okay. There was food on the table, we played a few sports, and life seemed good. They were actually starting to get on their feet financially. In fact, they started talking about buying a house when I was twelve. I remember my mum and dad always writing things down on paper, trying to figure out the math of it all. My dad would tally how many hours he'd worked, and how much he would get paid if he worked holidays and the odd weekend. Then they added Mum's salary to the equation, and suddenly it all seemed feasible. Every day became a game of guessing the probability of us getting a new house.

"Sixty percent, Dad?"

"Higher," he would answer.

"Seventy-five percent?" I would ask. Then we would spend a few minutes discussing why I would jump right from sixty to seventy-five before landing on his answer.

Finally, they put in an offer of $65,000 on a house at 325 Hollywood Avenue, about a mile away from where we lived. At that time, I knew nothing about offers and mortgages and everything that goes into buying a house. But I do remember how excited we all were. It was a small bungalow and it had an above-ground pool. It also had a big backyard where they would talk about having a vegetable and rose garden beside the pool. One day, I asked my dad what our chances of getting the house were.

"I'd say we've got about a thirty percent chance," he said.

A few days went by. There were more offers and counteroffers.

"Are we going to get the house?" I asked again.

"I'd say there's about a fifty percent possibility," he answered.

And then, somehow, it was ours. We all loved it. There was more space, things worked, and best of all, it was ours. My parents were so proud. To them, it was more than a place to live—it was proof that they had made it in a new country, after a lot of uncertainty and struggle. We packed up our things and moved. We put as much stuff in the car as we could, tied mattresses to the roof, walked as much stuff over as we could, and literally moved everything ourselves. Dad would joke about how good this was for our hockey conditioning. We didn't buy that, especially because my sister never played hockey.

My parents thought they would live in that house well into their old age. But Mum was working for a dentist who was a complete asshole. Eventually, my dad decided enough was enough and told her to quit. He wouldn't allow her to work for that man any longer. With interest rates on the rise to 18 percent, Dad couldn't renew the mortgage and had to sell the house. My parents were heartbroken. We moved back to 11 Elkhorn Drive.

After that, the zest seemed to go out of my mother. I think she was bored and lonely. Her children were at school all day, and when her husband wasn't at work, he was at the local Legion. Getting her hair done was a big event for her. My mother really liked to give cards to people. If I went to, say, the mall with her, I'd soon find a greeting card in the mailbox: "Thank you, son, for the lovely time at the mall yesterday." At the time, we all just thought she was really into greeting cards. I know better now. She sent them for everything, and I mean everything. If I sent her a note thanking her for the card, I would get another card soon, thanking me for the note. It was a "thank you card" cycle that was hard to break.

My brother went to Western Michigan University on a hockey scholarship. My sister couldn't afford to go to college. For some reason, she also didn't qualify for student loans because we owned the house on Hollywood Avenue at the time. Having inherited my father's reverence for the truth, she was no doubt unable to exaggerate her need for a grant. Some of her friends were way better off than us and still got grants and loans. It was a shame; she was the smartest of the three of us. Instead, she went to work at a bank, where she met her husband of now almost forty years, so it all worked out.

I went to York University, which we could only afford if I lived at home. On the day I was accepted, I found a note from my mother. I still have it, and I look at it from time to time. She told me how proud she was. She also told me that, with all of her children in university, she didn't know what she was going to do with herself. I wish I had read between the lines more. My mum was struggling with all of us being gone. It's a phase of my own life I'm currently dreading.

I hated my first year at university. It was an hour-long commute each way via public transportation. In my second year, I moved into residence, using money that I'd made working at The Keg (by eighteen, I was earning more than my father was at the TTC). Things got better, though I remained a terrible student. I slept through my morning classes, and changed my major every semester. It took me five years to graduate. In my final year, I applied to become a teacher through the physical education program at St. Francis Xavier University in Antigonish, Nova Scotia. I went in May, so as to work at a restaurant job I'd lined up for myself. My father took me to the airport. It was the only time I've seen him cry.

"Son," he said, "we're so proud of you," and he gave me a hug. Mum was crying as well. So was I. I sat at the gate and cried by myself some more. It must have been hard for them to see their last child move out. As a parent, I get it even more now.

As I've said, my father didn't find me that funny and didn't come to my shows. Which meant my mother didn't come to my shows, either. That's pretty much how things worked back then. This, I knew, was a disappointment. She was proud of me and wanted to see what I did. Sometime in 2003, I was headlining at the Yuk Yuk's in Mississauga, and she asked me if she could come to see me.

"Mum," I said, "I'd love you to see me work. There's one thing you should know. Some of the comics . . . well, they can get a little, you know . . . *racy*."

"What?" she said. "You think I was born yesterday?"

So I took her. When we arrived, I told her I still needed to work on some notes for my set, so I got her a good seat at the back while I continued to prepare. She was fine with this. The first comedian was my friend Frank Spadone. So funny, so nice. I had no doubt that she'd love him, and she did. Sure enough, about five minutes in, I could see her shoulders bobbing as she laughed. From time to time, she looked back and gave me a thumbs-up. I was so glad she was enjoying herself.

I was still at the back, scribbling away, when Spadone introduced the next comic: "Ladies and gentlemen, I give you . . . Terry Clement."

All I could think was *Oh, no*. Though very funny, Clement was probably the filthiest comic working the Canadian circuit at the time. I ran up to my mother. By this point, she was chatting happily with the people seated near her. I tapped on her shoulder. She turned.

"C'mon, Mum, this comic's not for you. Let's step out for a bit."

"Oh, get lost," she said in that thick Glaswegian accent of hers. "I'll be fine."

I sat with her. Clement came out. Back then, he had a very clean-cut, almost Howdy Doody–like appearance. This was deliberate, as it fooled the audience into letting their guard down. Grinning like a schoolboy, he started singing "When the Saints Go Marching In." Pretty soon, the whole audience was singing. My mother, who loved that song, was singing as well. Then, she was clapping. "Oh, how I long to be in that number, when the saints go marching in!" Meanwhile, I knew what was coming. I had worked with Terry many times before, and I knew his opening bit quite well.

Clement stopped singing. Everyone else stopped singing. He looked out over the audience with a mischievous grin. Then he yelled, as loudly as he could, "Who here loves to suck coooooock?!"

"Let's go," Mum said, and we went across the street to have a coffee.

It was unusual to be with her alone, in my thirties, like this. Though I can't remember what we talked about, I remember wishing I could do this with her more often—just hang out. I'd kill to have one more of those coffees with her.

A few years later, she had her first fall. I wasn't there, but it seems she lost her balance. She ended up badly smashing her face and suffering a concussion. Still, we didn't worry; she was seventy-two years old, and these things happen. Then she fell getting out of my sister's pool. Again, we didn't worry. Whose balance doesn't go a little when they age? Then her memory started to go. At first, the doctors thought her vertigo might have something to do with the fluid in her spine. They ran tests. Nothing showed up. She started having trouble swallowing. Her memory worsened. I remember the day when I knew it was starting to get really bad. She was home from the hospital and lying in her bed, where she spent most of her time by now. I dropped by for a visit to find her alone, watching the television. By sheer fluke, *Mr. D* was on. When I entered the room, she pointed at the television.

"Look, Gerry! It's a show about a teacher at a high school! He looks like you."

Dementia, in other words. Advanced Alzheimer's. What people don't realize is that dementia affects the entire body. She became immobile. She had trouble eating, until she couldn't eat at all without choking. Meanwhile, my father took care of her—inserting her feeding tube, keeping her comfortable. My siblings and I insisted that she needed professional care. Though he protested, we found a long-term care facility for her to live in. My father visited and decided that the place was insufficient. They didn't move her enough. They left her tube in too long. They didn't clean her enough. He took her out and cared for her at home. There was another care facility, and then another. Each time, he'd take her out. "Gerry," he'd tell me, "I can handle this."

She was at home for the entire year before she died on June 15, 2015.

That day, the phone rang. It was my father. He sounded frantic. "Gerry, something's wrong. It's your mother. She's not breathing well. I don't know what to do."

"Dad," I said, "I'll be right there." He had already called 911.

I called Kevin and Angela. Neither conversation lasted more than a minute. I couldn't find my keys. Finally, I did. I jumped in the car. I was at Yonge Street and the 401 when my phone rang. It was my father.

"Gerry," he said, "she's gone."

That was a Monday. I was due to fly to Halifax to shoot *Mr. D* on the Wednesday. I rescheduled. The funeral was on

Saturday. For the service, my brother and sister and I all made memory boards. Yet we all had the same problem: finding photos. We didn't take enough photos.

I went to Halifax on the Sunday to shoot *Mr. D.* In between takes, I'd go to my trailer and cry. Then I'd step out and be funny. It helped that I had a character to step into. My family, including my dad, came out for a vacation. Throughout, I was constantly taking pictures of my father. I wanted to make sure the memory board at *his* wake was a good one when his time came. He noticed, and I told him why. One day, after taking his picture, I said, "Hey, Dad, how's about changing your shirt, so that it looks like I took the same picture on two different days?" He thought that was hilarious. See, he did find me funny—just not onstage.

I was upset about my mother's death for the longest time. I thought often of those thank you cards she wrote, and wished I'd paid her and her words in those cards more attention. Not getting the chance to say goodbye? That still hurts. My mother's name was Alice. Two days after her death, my sister called me.

"You know what I just found out?" she said. "Mum died on the Feast Day of St. Alice. Can you believe that?" Mum died on the feast day of the saint she was named after. The odds were one in 365, or about a quarter of a percentage point. I'm a religious person, and I think she was sending me a little sign. I think she was telling me it was okay to let her go. This helped.

After my mum died, I felt an enormous amount of guilt, wondering if she really knew how much I loved her and how much she meant to me. I found the note I'd sent to her and my father back in 2003, when I was living in Los Angeles, and was comforted that I'd said a lot of those things back then. I also got a chance to say some more when she was ill. Not enough, but a little more. You never really know when you'll get a chance to say these things, so I'm glad I thought to put it in writing to both of them before I left for LA. The next time I would tell my mum how I felt about her was when I read her eulogy at her funeral in 2015. It was the hardest speech I've ever given.

When I think of my mum, I think of how much she loved to laugh. And dance. They would often go hand in hand. She was so happy when she danced, and even happier if I joined in. I guess my love of dancing comes from her. Although I haven't mastered the dancing and laughing at the same time yet.

As for my father, he still lives in a condo we bought for him and Mum in 2006. Each time I see him, I try to take some pictures or videos of him and my kids. I want lots of memories. As much as I knew that my parents dying was a part of life, I never allowed myself to prepare for it. It never feels real. Losing my mum taught me so much about being a parent. Enjoy the little moments, as they are the ones you will remember the most. Like having a coffee together for twenty minutes at Tim Hortons.

About two weeks ago, I was driving my fifteen-year-old daughter, Alyce, to a volleyball game. We didn't know the area very well. For some reason, on the drive I started talking about my mum to her. She got to know her nana a little bit. We were trying to find somewhere to eat. I pulled onto Dixie Road and into a mall that seemed to have a lot of food choices. As I looked to my left, there was a Tim Hortons beside me. I looked around and realized it was the same Tim Hortons across from the Yuk Yuk's where my mum saw me perform. The same one where we sat and talked for twenty minutes about anything. I smiled as I thought of her and that conversation we had about eighteen years earlier. It made my day.

I miss her so much.

# ILLNESS AND ME

**W**hile my dad was working as a police officer in Glasgow, a serial killer named Peter Manuel was on the loose in Scotland. Branded the "Beast of Birkenshaw" by the press, he was later convicted of killing seven people, though police believe there may have been others. As punishment, he became the second-last person to be hanged at Glasgow's Barlinnie prison.

Today, my father is eighty-nine years old, and he can still remember the names of every one of Manuel's victims. Growing up, we constantly heard about Manuel, as well as every other serial killer on the loose. Son of Sam, John Wayne Gacy, Jeffrey Dahmer, Clifford Olson—these were all familiar names at the Donoghue dinner table. He was also obsessed with the Emanuel Jaques case. Jaques was a Portuguese shoeshine boy who was murdered in some seedy apartment above a Yonge Street massage parlour in

Toronto. "Don't *ever*," Dad would say, "go to Yonge Street. Do you understand?"

When I was young, a boy fell off a bridge near where we lived and drowned. This made an impression on my father. Every time I wanted to do anything, he reminded me of people who had been murdered, drowned, died in a fire or been kidnapped. In his mind, anything that happened in the news, anywhere in the world, past or present, could happen to *me*.

So, I blame my father for my hypochondria.

I had gone to driving ranges and knew golf was a sport I really wanted to try. The first time I played an actual round of golf was when I was twelve. I knew I needed to ask for permission because I'd be gone all day. So I called up my father.

"Hi, son," he said in his thick Scottish brogue.

"Hi, Dad," I said. "Alan wants me to go golfing with him and his brother. Can I go?"

There was a long silence. I could guess what was coming. The only thing I didn't know was what his reasoning might be.

"Hemmm," he said. "I don't think so."

"Why not?"

"It's too dangerous."

"*Dad*," I pleaded. "What's dangerous about golf?"

"Now, you know as well as I do, son, that Peter Manuel nabbed one of his victims on a golf course. Like I say, it's just too dangerous. There's also lots of ponds and rivers on the course. So, no. You come home. You come home right away."

I hung up. I couldn't even tell Alan and James why my dad had said no. At twelve years old, even I knew how stupid it was. I decided to call my dad back. I was pacing before the call; for the first time in my life, I was about to defy him. "Dad, that's ridiculous, that makes no sense. I'm going to go golfing!"

I heard a pause in his voice. "Fine," he said, "but be careful."

And the thing was, it *was* ridiculous. Peter Manuel killed people in the 1950s. In Scotland. He'd been dead for decades. Still, in my father's mind, there *could* be another Peter Manuel, just waiting in the woods at Don Valley Golf Course, preparing for his first kill, rubbing his hands with a pre-murderous glee, on the exact day that his son, one Gerry Donoghue, decided to try golfing for the first time.

Another example. I was twenty-three, and about to go to Cancún with a friend of mine. The night before we were leaving, my phone rang. It was my father.

"Gerry!" he said, clearly concerned.

"What is it?"

"I've just watched a documentary about scorpions. Do you know about scorpions?"

"Not really."

"Horrible things. If they sting you, you've got minutes to live. And the thing is, Gerry, *they have them in Mexico.*"

"Dad, please . . ."

"And you know, Gerry, they're sneaky little buggers. They can hide in your sheets, or in your shoes. So, promise me that when you get to your hotel room, the first thing you do is pull your sheets off the bed and check for scorpions. Then, in the morning, make sure you dump out your shoes before you put them on."

"I will, Dad."

"Because they can kill you, they really can. Oh, and have fun. Bye, son."

The problem, as far as I can tell, is that he reads things in newspapers, or sees things on television, and it triggers the part of his brain that is still, on some subconscious level, afraid of Peter Manuel. Most noticeably, it flares up every time I go to the United States.

"Gerry," he'll say, "you be careful down there."

"I will."

"No . . . you be *very* careful. There are a lot of bad people down there."

"Dad, there are bad people everywhere."

"Ahhh, but not like in the United States. They all have guns down there, Gerry, so things can turn murderous at the blink of an eye. So, you be careful."

"I will, Dad."

"Good. Have a nice trip."

So, there it is. I grew up bombarded by catastrophic thinking. While I knew that my father's fears were absurd, that my chances of being butchered by a homicidal maniac on a golf course were slim at best, I still inherited the sort of worry that leads to those conclusions. I just chose to apply it in another way. I went looking for something that really could get me, and the thing I came up with, time and time again, was illness.

While I was pretty sure that Peter Manuel wasn't hiding on golf courses, health problems really *did* exist. I became fascinated with anything to do with health, or the body, or the medical world. As a kid, I memorized the names of body parts. I learned medical terminology, never dreaming that I was preparing for my life as a hypochondriac. I even wanted to become a doctor, which I knew would be a problem, as I was a C student in high school, and C students were not admitted to medical school. As I mentioned earlier, I applied to McMaster in Hamilton, the only med school in Canada that didn't require you to write the MCAT. I filled out my application the night before it was due. I did not get in.

Instead, I twinned my interest in all things medical with my father's irrational suspicions and became a man who, for one endless weekend, became convinced he had some rare disease. It was not an isolated event. One day, my hand started to shake, just a little, and I became convinced that I was displaying an early sign of something bad. I was not. After having a severe migraine, I worried that I was having an aneurysm. I went to the emergency department for tests. I was able to book an MRI on my brain (this was difficult, as I am also claustrophobic—I had to take an Ativan to get through the procedure). I was fine. I've had more COVID tests than I've had good meals, and for a considerable period of time, I was convinced I had long COVID. I have also undergone genetic testing, in which I paid to check for the presence of 132 genetic defects that are known to cause health problems. I had none of them.

I own a stethoscope and one of those little hand-held lights that doctors shine into the noses and ears of patients. I don't know how to use them, but I own them. In our house, I even have a dedicated spot for our thermometer; if my wife uses it and forgets to put it back in its rightful spot, I get annoyed. So, yes, I'm always checking for symptoms, for lumps, for a weird pulse, for tremors and twitches and unusual sores. On myself or my kids. Trust me: every skin blemish is a melanoma, every ache a harbinger of doom. In fact, I don't even *need* symptoms to become alarmed. Once, I read an article that said that, by the time you experience any symptoms associated with pancreatic cancer, it's too late. That one scares me the most.

My worst instance of hypochondria-related panic came in July of 2011. At the time, I was filming *Mr. D* in Nova Scotia. As part of some charity event I'd attended, I had auctioned off a visit to the set, as well as lunch with the star of the show—which, in this case, was me. The top bidders, a nice couple I'll call Dave and Lisa, were from Halifax. Both of them looked like young, healthy individuals. I remember sitting down with them at the *Mr. D* lunch table as we talked about the show and what it is like filming it every day. I told them how great it was, but that it was tough on days when I felt tired.

"Some days," I told them, "I feel tired all the time. Maybe it's just part of being in your forties."

Without missing a beat, Dave looked at me with a curious expression and said, "You might have Lyme disease."

"Sorry?" I asked. "Lyme disease?"

"Yes. Lyme disease," Lisa said. "It's caused when an infected tick bites—"

"Lisa and I have both had it. In fact, we both still have it. It doesn't go away, you know. And fatigue is one of the biggest symptoms."

"That's funny. I was coming home from golfing about a month ago, and this bug landed on my hand. I just shooed it away."

"Yes, but did it bite you?"

"Uhhh, I don't think so. I didn't think anything of it at the time."

"It probably bit you. Sometimes you don't feel the bite. It's so quick."

"Mmmm . . . I don't think it did. But it might have. Either way, I really don't think I have Lyme disease. I'm just a bad sleeper. I didn't sleep well last night. That's why I'm tired."

Both Dave and Lisa shook their heads, as if to indicate they were privy to knowledge that I, a brand new Lyme disease sufferer, was not. "It sounds like Lyme disease," Dave said once again.

"Yes," agreed Lisa. "It's Lyme disease all right."

"I'll tell you what," Dave said. "I'll give you my email address. If the symptoms persist, feel free to ask me questions. As Lyme disease sufferers, Lisa and I have done a lot of research."

He gave me his email address. I took it, not realizing that one of the worst things that can ever happen to a hypochondriac had just happened.

My fatigue continued. I started to get headaches. They weren't serious headaches, but, given the possibility that I was ill with a tick-borne parasite, I thought it might be significant. I emailed Dave and told him that, in addition to being tired, I was starting to get some minor headaches.

"I really think you should get it checked out."

My fatigue and headaches didn't go away. Then my hip started to hurt. At first, I thought little of it—an old hockey injury, no doubt, or maybe I'd tweaked it playing golf. I still played squash back then, and squash is murder on the hips. So I stopped playing squash. The pain persisted, the day soon coming when I realized that my mild hip pain had somehow graduated into moderate hip pain and would, if left untreated, no doubt graduate into severe hip pain.

I emailed Dave.

"My hip hurts," I told him.

"How much?"

"A fair bit."

"That's not good. Muscle pain, joint pain, cartilage pain . . ."

"My God," I said, trying to sound at least partially composed. "I have all three!"

"Gerry. I mean it. Get it checked out."

"But I read online that, when you have Lyme disease, you get a sort of bull's eye–shaped rash. I don't have any kind of rash."

"No! That's wrong! The vast majority of people get a rash. But not all. Lisa, for example, never had a bull's eye rash, and she suffers terribly." Two weeks earlier, I had never heard anyone say "Lyme disease." I had now heard it three hundred times in a matter of days.

This was all I needed to hear. If you are a hypochondriac, you are never one of the vast majority of people who, suffering from fatigue, slept poorly the night before. You are never a person who, suffering from bloating and minor stomach upset, simply ate something that disagreed with them. You are never a person who, suffering from low-level vertigo, could simply do with a vacation. Oh, no—you are one of the special people, saddled with undiagnosed leukemia, or stomach cancer, or brain tumours, or all three. In my case, I was one of those rare individuals who contract Lyme disease without a rash. Apparently, it happens less than two percent of the time.

My insomnia worsened. Every night, I'd wake up at 3 a.m. and start pacing. So as to not wake the rest of my family during such periods, I often sleep in a spare room in the basement. One day, I saw a bug down there, on the floor, *where it could have easily bitten me on my feet.* So I trapped it. I put it in one of those little sealed plastic baggies that are just big enough to hold, say, an extracted molar. I didn't even wait till morning to email Dave.

"I think I found the culprit," I typed.

"What do you mean?"

"There was a bug, on my basement floor."

"Hmm. That's not good. What's it look like?"

"Small, round, black."

"How many legs?"

"Uhhh . . . hard to say . . . eight?"

"It's a tick. Gerry, you *have* to get tested."

"I will, I will."

"But listen: don't go to your doctor. Regular doctors, they know very little about Lyme disease and testing for it. Lisa's doctor gave her a false negative."

"Really?"

"Really. We *both* got false negatives, in fact. There's only one place on earth that will give you a really thorough test. It specializes in testing for tick-borne diseases. Personally, I wouldn't trust anybody else."

"Okay, okay, where is it?"

"Germany."

"I have to go to Germany?"

"Of course not. You just send them a blood sample. It's really quite convenient."

I contacted the lab. I gave them eight hundred dollars. In return, they sent me a little blood collection kit, along with instructions. I booked an appointment at a lab that could extract the blood for me. Then I sent some of my blood to Germany. A week or two later, they emailed me to say that the blood sample had expired and that I needed to send them another sample. This was no problem; the kit came with several vials for just such an eventuality. I mailed them another sample.

Then I waited. I was still sleeping in the basement. Often, when I woke up at three in the morning and didn't feel like pacing, I'd look at my phone. I'd watch YouTube videos, read Twitter or catch up on the news. I'd also check my email. There it was. My results from the esteemed lab in

Germany. I opened the email, thinking the results would state categorically whether I had, or did not have, Lyme disease. Instead, I was met with a chart that listed about a thousand bodily substances—enzymes, corpuscles, bacteria, proteins, lipids, the list went on and on. Beside each substance was a number. If those numbers were too high or too low, they appeared in red. I had three red numbers that were slightly high. I went to the internet and looked up my first red number. There it was: my CD57+ NK cells (absolute) were 0.61/μL. I had no idea what these numbers, units and letters stood for, but I did know that I had the disease. I didn't bother looking up the other two red numbers.

I still remember sitting on the side of the bed, looking down, my heart pounding, thinking, *I have Lyme disease*. I hadn't caught it in time. I would suffer for the rest of my life. My brain would swell, I'd get a permanent fever and I'd start forgetting where I lived. Immediately, I started doing research, my thumbs hammering against my phone.

I didn't sleep that night. In the morning, I phoned my doctor's office, pleading with his assistant that I'd had some very bad medical news and that I needed to see him immediately. She got me an appointment. I went in. My doctor looked at the blood results.

"Gerry," he said, "you do not have Lyme disease."

Now I had another problem. Who to believe? On the side of my having Lyme disease were Dave, Lisa, Germany and the full weight of the internet. On the side of my *not* having Lyme disease was my GP, whom I'd seen for years. Then it occurred to me: the sides weren't evenly numbered.

It would be unfair to judge at this point. So, I talked to more doctors, a naturopath or two, and an osteopath who treated me for my hip pain. Gradually, they all talked me down. And then I found this on the internet: CD57 testing for Lyme disease is meaningless and a waste of money. I got a good night's sleep and took Extra-Strength Tylenol. My Lyme disease went away. I had beaten it. At least, that's what it felt like.

The worst part of my hypochondria? I am doing exactly what my father did to me. I am passing it along to my children. I can't tell you how many times I've taken them to emergency because I was worried about a productive cough. After they play sports, if they complain about anything to do with their breathing or heartbeat, I pull out my stethoscope and listen to their lungs or their heartbeat. I don't know what I'm listening for, but I'm still listening. I don't even know what a murmur sounds like. And yet, there I am, listening, hoping, praying. I also check for unusual bruising, for fatty tissue deposits, for unexplained sores.

The other day, my daughter came up to me and asked me if the rash on her arm was Lyme disease. I made light of it. Meanwhile, I was thinking, *This is all my fault.* But that's the thing about hypochondria—it's a full-time job. You spend an insane amount of time in waiting rooms, in doctor's offices, in pediatric clinics. Other than providing material for the odd bit, hypochondria is also terrible for my work. Recently, while filming *Family Feud Canada*, I got a call from my twelve-year-old daughter, who said she'd come down with a headache. I phoned her at the next commercial break. She said she was seeing double. Now I was really worried. She was home alone. When I called her at the next break, she didn't answer. (I later learned that she was asleep.) Now I went crazy. I called my wife and begged her to race home. Meanwhile, I couldn't think, much less be funny. The producers asked if I was okay. I told them I was. I wasn't. My daughter's name is Faith. One of the contestants that day was named Faith. I became convinced that this was no coincidence, that it was some sort of demonic harbinger of this horrible *thing*, whatever it was, that had gotten its claws into my middle child.

And you would think, given the severity of my hypochondria, that I might have received some sort of therapy, that I might have joined a support group for sufferers of hypochondria, or, at the very least, gotten myself a prescription for some sort of anxiety-relieving medication. If I haven't, it's only because my hypochondria has gotten slightly better of late. Am I saner? Healthier? More balanced? Unlikely. If I've experienced any alleviation of symptoms, it's because I've already had every test in the book. I've had MRIs, CAT scans, ultrasounds, genetic exams and X-rays galore. I've had every part of me poked and prodded, every bodily fluid tested and retested. As a result, I've started to run out of illnesses to assign myself. This has helped. I'm in hypochondria remission.

Yet I also know that my hypochondria is always out there, waiting to return. When it does, I know its tactics will be imaginative. Once when I was performing in Kingston,

Ontario, as I let myself into my hotel room, I looked at the locks on the inside of the door. *Of course*, I thought, I'll *use the main lock*. The hotel staff all have keys, and they can get in if they really need to. But the door also had one of those locks—they look a little like a fence latch—that can only be opened from the inside. *Do I use it?* I asked myself. *Do I?* What if I get terribly ill and call for help, but can't get out of bed to open the door for the paramedics? What then, Gerry Dee?

So I never put the extra lock on hotel doors. According to my father, this means I could get murdered easily, but at least if I have something go wrong, the paramedics can still get into the room. It's safe, smart and, best of all, hypochondria-proof.

# MIGRAINES

My older brother got migraines. My older sister got migraines. I can remember my mother, curled up in a dark room, moaning. The only person in my family who didn't get migraines was my father. Yet, with all of the people around him who, on a regular basis, held their heads while promising that they were about to throw up, he was sympathetic.

I got my first when I was fourteen. This is not uncommon. It was a Saturday, I believe (though it could have been a Sunday; all I remember is that it didn't get me out of going to school). I woke up with a headache that day, which was par for the course for those who came from the Coogan side of the family. By noon, I was back in bed, holding my head, thinking this was the worst headache I'd ever had. It only got worse from there: I was nauseous, noises bothered me, I couldn't concentrate, talking was hard, and any kind of bright light was unbearable.

I went to my father. He was in the living room, reading his newspaper. I must have looked terrible: hunched over, blinking, paper-white, groaning, holding whatever part of my head was pounding through my skull. Migraine sufferers tend to experience pain in a specific part of the brain: at migraine support meetings, you'll hear people identify as a right-brain sufferer or a left-brain sufferer. I'm as liable to get them on the left side as the right side. I get them in the front—they're awful, as it feels as though your eyeballs are about to pop out—and I get them in the back of the head. I even get them at the back of the neck, which is highly unusual, as the neck is not technically part of the head.

"Ah," Dad said. "You might have a migraine."

I winced. He walked over to the kitchen counter and handed me a pill. "Take this. It will help with the pain."

"I don't know if I can swallow this," I told him.

"What do you mean? It's a wee pill. Put it in your mouth and drink some water. It will just go down on its own."

"But Mum usually crushes them."

"Crushes what?"

"The pill! She crushes it for me and puts it on a spoon with a little juice to help me swallow it."

He just stared at me. He wasn't impressed. This former Glasgow police officer would have none of this. I was somewhat surprised that he was so angry. Yet I was also surprised that he had never wondered how Mum had gotten me to ingest medicine for all these years. And so, I tried. At first, he was kind and caring and understanding.

"Just put it toward the back of your tongue, take a sip of water and swallow."

I followed the instructions to a T. No such luck. I thought I'd swallowed it, but I hadn't. I pulled out the now-soggy pill and held it in my fingers.

"C'mon, just put it in your mouth and swallow it," he ordered, his Scottish accent getting thicker and louder. The caring part was slowly disappearing.

I tried again, only to gag and present the pill as if I had just pulled a splinter out of my mouth. I couldn't do it. He was not amused. How could a fourteen-year-old child not swallow a pill that was just a quarter of an inch in diameter? By now, Mum had entered to witness this pill-swallowing debacle. She weighed in as well. It didn't help. Dad stormed off, disgusted that his youngest child, just two years away from getting a driver's licence, couldn't swallow a pill. Mum stayed and tried to help. We had to get a new pill, since the one I'd started with had now pretty much dissolved in my hand. I still couldn't do it. The gag reflex kept coming. I asked her to crush it and she refused. At the same time, my head was pounding more and more from my migraine. I was also crying, both from the pain in my head and from having humiliated myself in front of my father, who was now coming back down the stairs.

"Here he comes," Mum burst out. "Quick!" I put the pill in my mouth and drank and drank and drank. Water went everywhere. Down my cheeks, down my shirt and on the floor—it seems I had been born with a reflex in my mouth that didn't let an object enter my esophagus at the same time as a liquid. I knew I was running out of time as Dad drew closer.

"Hurry!" Mum cheered.

Each time I thought I'd swallowed it, I hadn't. Dad was getting closer. I could hear his loud Scottish footsteps. And then, finally, as he entered the kitchen, I did it. I swallowed the pill. Mum let out a big smile.

"Dad!" I exclaimed. "I did it. I swallowed the pill!"

"Big deal," he said.

Twenty minutes later, my headache was gone. Yet it had been replaced with chest pains, stomach pains, a speeding pulse, vomiting and an overwhelming sensation of dread. So I went back to my dad.

"What did you give me?"

"Tylenol 3."

It turns out my mum had always taken Tylenol 3 for *her* migraines, so my dad thought it would be good for mine as well. It made sense: regular-strength Tylenol wouldn't touch the pain of a migraine. As the pain increased in my chest, we decided to go to the emergency room. Nobody really knew what the problem was, but we decided it must have been a reaction to the Tylenol with codeine. By the end of the day, I was an expert on codeine, migraines and pill swallowing.

What's the best way to tell the difference between a migraine and a severe headache? When you take yourself to the hospital, moaning in agony, and you are given a pain magnitude test, and you respond with a number that is high enough to qualify for the category known as "exquisite," then chances are you're experiencing a migraine. And yet, for the next eight years or so, I was spared this horror. Don't get me wrong, I had lots of headaches. I had them in the morning, and in the evening. I had them during times of stress, and on the rare occasions my family took a holiday. They came without rhyme or reason. I suppose I'm just a headachy guy. Even now, as I write this, I have a headache. I'm also getting nervous that all this talk about migraines will cause my headache to vault into "exquisite" territory.

But I'm getting ahead of myself. My next migraine happened when I was at St. Francis Xavier University, studying to become a teacher. One night, I went out drinking with my roommates. By the time we got home, I was fully expecting to get the headache I always used to get when I drank alcohol. (It's one of the reasons I don't drink today.)

As any migraine sufferer knows, there is that moment when your everyday, run-of-the-mill headache veers into the realm of the extreme. Suddenly, you can feel all the symptoms associated with a migraine gathering in the distance, preparing to charge—I'm talking about nausea, confusion, listlessness, light sensitivity, noise sensitivity and a score of ten on the pain magnitude test. Yet, what people never talk about is the fear that comes when that moment is reached, the absolute terror that your day will no longer be one in which you're merely bothered by a sore head, and is about to become one where you are stuck in bed, in a dark room, whimpering.

So, yes—my headache was becoming worse. From what I remember, it was on the left side of my head, yet was also blooming across my forehead. These types of migraines, the ones that cover not one but two zones, were the worst. I walked into Brendan's room—he was one of my roommates—and asked if he had any Tylenol. He handed me two pills that he pulled out of a bottle with no label on it.

"Are you sure these are Tylenol?" I asked.

"Yes, they are. I also have some Advil in here if you want." Apparently, Brendan didn't like to keep his pills in the original bottle; instead, he mixed them into his own little bottle and played "find the medicine" each time he needed a pill.

I took the Tylenol—Mum always told me that Advil wasn't as good for your stomach.

Twenty minutes later, the pain in my head, if not vanished altogether, had definitely gone down a few knots. At the same time, I was beginning to experience a pain in my chest—the same pain I'd had when my father gave me Tylenol 3s. I went back to Brendan and asked him what he gave me.

"Tylenol."

"Regular Tylenol?"

"I think so. Could be Tylenol 3s, though. I keep a couple of them in there in case."

*Oh boy*, I thought.

I drove myself to Antigonish General Hospital. There, a nurse hooked me up to a heart monitor. My pulse had reached 245 beats per minute. The pain in my chest was scary. A doctor came in. He asked about my symptoms. I described them all. As before, there was confusion and concern as to what was causing this chest pain and vomiting. He conducted a bunch of tests and waited. Everything seemed normal. The doctor, after a thorough check of my history, confirmed that I was allergic to codeine. I remember his last words before I left.

"So, whatever you do, the next time you have a migraine, do *not* take any pain medication with codeine in it."

"I won't," I told him, but did so anyway.

It happened in Windsor, Ontario. I was visiting a buddy of mine, and we'd gone out for a few drinks. I woke up with a pounding headache. Was it a migraine? I wasn't sure. I asked my buddy, "Do you have anything?"

"Some Tylenol."

"Regular Tylenol?"

"Yup," he said.

I popped two into my mouth. I didn't even need water to swallow pills anymore. I was a pro now; you build up some saliva, and down they go. By the time they entered my esophagus, I grabbed the bottle to make sure it was regular Tylenol. I should have done this before, but why would my friend lie to me? After all, we were in our mid-twenties. We all knew what regular Tylenol was, right? I looked at the bottle.

"Tylenol 1" was written on the side.

"What does that mean, 'Tylenol 1'?" I asked.

"I got them in Detroit. I think that's just what they call their regular Tylenol."

I kept reading the label. Nope. "Tylenol 1" meant it contained codeine. Less codeine than Tylenol 3, but codeine nonetheless. I remember the fear I experienced when I saw the words *with Codeine* in small print. I jumped up and sped to the hospital. There, I told the emergency room physicians that I was deadly allergic to codeine, and they brought me right in. "Deadly" might have been a bit dramatic, but I knew the chest pain and vomiting were about to start soon. And they did.

After that, I pretty much settled into my life as a chronic migraine sufferer. On a typical migraine day, I'll wake up with a headache, and by noon I'll have a migraine. Then I'll go to bed for the rest of the day—migraine sufferers do love a dark room. But if I had a gig, I did it anyway—the show must go on. If you're the headliner, the people have paid to see *you*. So you can't send a substitute. All you can do is tough it out. In my career, it's happened about five times. I wish I could say that I've developed coping mechanisms for when I'm onstage with a migraine. But really, there's nothing you can do. You can't think. It's hard to remember the material. The sound of the audience laughing? It's a chainsaw. Those floodlights shining in your eyes? It's torture. I remember one night, onstage, my head splitting, having just thrown up, I said out loud, "I tell ya, folks, if I'm a little off tonight, it's because I've got one hell of a migraine." I think they thought it was a bit.

With time, I've figured out what my triggers are. A lack of exercise is one of them. Lack of sleep is another. I have to make sure I drink enough water. Stress? Yes, of course, it goes without saying. Bad food is another big one, which is difficult, as I've always been one of the world's worst eaters. Looking back, it's no wonder I got headaches all the time as a kid. Later, when I started flying to gigs, I noticed that every time I ate airplane food, I'd get a migraine. I think it's all the sodium. So I started making sure I ate a big meal before a flight and then turning down any food on board. Chocolate and gummy bears definitely can cause my migraines. Too bad. I'm not giving up chocolate and gummy bears. I'll suffer.

As every migraine sufferer knows, there are dozens of things you can do to treat a migraine, none of which work all that well. Many find that a cup of coffee, if consumed at a critical moment in the onset of your migraine, helps. It doesn't for me. I find that heating pads, applied to the head, do; at my house, you'll find them lying around all over the place, always at arm's length. I find that standing in a hot shower helps (though, again, only a little).

Thinking that my migraines are actually the consequence of a brain tumour, I've had more tests than I care to admit to. Thankfully, there is a new non-narcotic, migraine-specific medication that usually works: at present, I have some in my truck, in my office, in my backpack and in my golf bag. Why? I've learned the hard way that you can never have too much of the stuff lying around.

Once, in the middle of the night, I woke with a migraine. It was exactly 1:55 in the morning. I went to the bathroom to fetch one of my pills. There were none. I remembered that I had some in my truck. So I headed outside, in my boxer shorts and a hoodie, to fetch my medication. Thank God I had some. There's nothing worse than running out of the medication. Keeping a few in my car turned out to be a great idea.

The next morning, I went outside to take my kids to school. My neighbour was in his driveway, talking to the police. I went over to see what had happened. It turned out that someone had stolen his SUV in the middle of the night. The police asked me if I'd seen anything. I told them I hadn't. "But," I said, "I've got security cameras on the outside of my house. It might have picked up something. If you'd like, I could go back inside and have a look."

I went inside and started scrolling through the footage. Sure enough, he was there, a grainy stranger. He'd tried to get into my truck as well! I wondered why he hadn't stolen my truck instead of my neighbour's. Did I have better security in my car? Maybe, maybe not. But then I saw the guy walk toward the front of my house. Turns out that he'd also tried to get into my house. *The bastard*, I thought, *thank God he hadn't*—fighting off a criminal in the middle of the night with a migraine would not have ended well for me or my family. I promised myself I'd install another camera, one that could film people *at* the front door. I'd also put in another lock or two—clearly, you couldn't be too careful. I went to pull the clip from the video, so that I could give it to the police. Then I noticed the time stamp—1:55 in the morning. The man in the footage was me. I had totally forgotten that I left the house to go to my car. I'd come *this* close to handing the police a video clip of myself, fetching my migraine medication in the middle of the night, and saying, "There ya go, officer, there's your man." It wasn't much help for my neighbour, but it did make me realize the cameras I had were awful.

So, there are things you can do. Here's the rub: by the time you notice you're getting a migraine, it's usually too late. I recently read an article about how they're training dogs to smell the hormonal changes that precede a migraine, the idea being that, if Rover starts barking like hell, it's time to have your coffee, or stand in a hot shower, or apply heating pads, or take whatever medication you happen to favour.

On the topic of medication, I'm now using a subcutaneous form of my favourite drug. That means I can simply inject myself in my ass cheek to get the medication to work faster. This stuff, at least for me, works. And yet, this is what migraines have done for me. They have turned me into a man who, without any hesitation or squeamishness, can drop his pants, reach around and jab a needle into his glute.

In fact, I remember the first time I had an injection of this magical concoction. It was twenty years ago now, and I had a corporate gig in London, Ontario. I woke up with a headache. By noon, it was a lot, lot worse. I was now facing a two-hour drive, as well as the prospect of performing. While I can't remember the name of the company that had hired me, I do remember that it was a Christmas party. Though I wanted to cancel, I knew they wouldn't be able to find a replacement on such short notice, and I didn't want to ruin their festivities and lose the gig.

So I went. It was a snowy day. Before getting on the highway, I pulled over at a Tim Hortons to get a cup of coffee. I didn't drink it. Instead, I held it to the side of my head; the warmth helped, though only a little. When the coffee got cold, I pulled over and bought another. You wouldn't believe how many Tim Hortons there are in southwestern Ontario. By the time I was nearing London, my migraine had gone beyond exquisite. I'd never known such pain. I pulled over and threw up. Sometimes, vomiting can help. This time, it didn't. The pain grew even worse: I was worried I might pass out—or, even worse, die (see "Illness and Me"). Was it a migraine or was it an aneurysm?

Exactly forty minutes from my gig, I spotted a hospital. I pulled over and ran into emergency. Luckily, I got in fairly quickly—I didn't even need my "I may have taken codeine and I have a deadly reaction to it" speech. I told them I was having a furious migraine and that I needed to give a presentation in a half-hour. I waited a bit. A doctor came. He told me to loosen my pants and bend over. I didn't argue. I felt the needle go in. Three minutes later, I felt fine.

"You're going to have to stay for some follow-up tests," a nurse told me.

"Okay," I told her.

She walked away, and I ran out of the hospital. Fifteen minutes later, I was onstage, doing my set in front of a room full of people holding cups of eggnog. If I remember correctly, I'm pretty sure I was funny.

# KIDS

One summer, when I was in Halifax shooting *Mr. D*, the whole family came out for a visit. On one of my days off, we went to a small fair in downtown Halifax. We were doing anything we could to entertain our three kids, who were all under the age of eight. At one point, my wife and I were talking to a father we'd met at the soccer camp the kids had attended a week earlier. Just then, our youngest daughter, Faith, came up to us. She, by the way, is known to have the quickest wit in our family, which also means that she's the sauciest in our family.

"Oh, Faith," I said, "this is so-and-so. So-and-so, this is Faith. She's one of our daughters."

"Hello," he said.

"Hi," she said.

"Are you having a good time?" he asked.

"So far," she answered.

"Are you going to go on the roller coasters?"

She looked at him, eyes widened, leaning back on her heels. "What are you," she asked, "drunk?"

She wandered off. The dad looked at me. I stood there, embarrassed.

Here is my point.

While the response "What are you, drunk?" is sort of funny (at best) when coming from the mouth of an adult, it sounds nothing but bratty when coming from the mouth of a kid who hasn't yet started Grade 1. Yet it wasn't her fault. She had heard that phrase so many times around the house. It's a Cape Breton thing. My wife's from Glace Bay, and there you say, "What're you, drunk?" in the same way that, in the rest of the English-speaking world, you might say, "What're you, nuts?" or "What're you, crazy?"

So, yes, it was our doing. Though your children don't become replicas of you, they do become like you, whether you want them to or not. In our case, my wife and I didn't know what we were doing. We didn't read any parenting books, we never watched any videos, we never visited any websites. It was chaos from the very beginning. Actually, it was chaos from *before* the beginning.

I was thirty-seven when Heather and I got married. Thirty-seven, as far as I'm concerned, is pushing the envelope where starting a family is concerned. No one wants to be that dad who can't play catch with his kids because it aggravates his back. As long as I can remember, I'd always wanted children. Even as a teenager, I'd start sentences with

"When I have children, I'm going to. . ." What teenage boy talks like that? I did, is the answer. That kid was me.

So, we didn't waste any time. If we were ill prepared for life with a baby, I blame haste. We were married on August 5, 2006. Within three months, Heather was pregnant. Her pregnancy was unremarkable, in that it wasn't particularly bad and it wasn't particularly good. Though she didn't throw up that much, she did throw up a little. Though she wasn't exhausted, neither was she one of those pregnant women who, by the third trimester, find themselves bursting with energy. Her due date, coincidentally, was August 5, 2007. Leading up to that date, I was in Los Angeles, filming *Last Comic Standing*. The plan was that, on August 1, I'd have a break in filming and would fly to Cape Breton, where my wife had decided to have the baby, and where her parents could help out. (Her mother's anxiety meant coming to Toronto was out of the question. My own parents were elderly—and, quite frankly, weren't *Heather's* parents.)

I was lying by a pool on July 28 when my brother-in-law called me. (His name, by the way, is Jerry. He was named after his father. My name, while spelled differently, sounds exactly the same. And so, at a family barbecue, if someone calls out, "Hey, Jerry, you want another hot dog?" it's more than likely that three heads will turn and answer, "Sure, why not?")

"Gerry?" he said.

"Yes?"

"It's Jerry."

"Hi, Jerry."

271

"Heather's in labour."

"What?"

"She's in labour."

Her mum and dad got her to the car and they made the short trip to the Glace Bay hospital. It turned out that she'd reached ten centimetres of dilation, and, as such, the pain was unbearable. The moment she got to the hospital, her water broke.

"So, when . . ."

"It's anybody's guess now, Gerry. You keep your phone with you, okay?"

An hour later, it rang again.

"Well," Jerry said, "you's got yourself a girl!"

I sat down and wept.

An hour later, I had to go back to work.

Aly was three days old when I was finally able to fly to Cape Breton and meet her. A few days later, we all flew back to Toronto, but I had to do another round of filming in LA right away. When that was over, I came home again, but a few days after *that*, I had to leave for the sixty-city tour required of the top five finishers on *Last Comic Standing*. Heather and Aly went back to Glace Bay to get settled while I finished the tour. Over the next three months, I had brief periods off, so I'd fly to Glace Bay through Halifax, usually on an overnight flight, and get home at 6 a.m. to help out where I could and see my wife and new daughter. But this didn't happen very often, and it never happened for very long—a few days at the most. Then I'd be back on an airplane.

This leads me to my second failing as a parent: I was oblivious. I just didn't realize what Heather was going through. Like a lot of newborn babies, Aly didn't sleep well and cried a lot. And yet, whenever Heather and I talked on the phone, I'd find some new way to be insensitive.

"I'm so tired," I'd say. "After last's night show, the promoters insisted that we go to some club. It was almost dawn before we got home."

Or: "God, my back hurts. I think I'm going to have to get a massage."

Or: "Yesterday, we were on the bus for nine hours. I've never been so bored. I thought I was going out of my mind."

I was completely unaware of how tough it was for her. The bottom line? I was a first-time dad who didn't have a clue how difficult it was to look after a baby without your partner.

After six months, Heather went back to work. She taught chemistry at the same high school where I'd taught history and phys. ed. This meant we needed someone to look after Aly. We found a woman named Mary. She was highly competent and came well recommended. I was the one who took Aly to Mary's house on the first day. Immediately, I flew into a panic: there were no baby gates at the top of the stairs—I'd had carpenters come to our home and install them. I mentioned this to her as I struggled to maintain my composure.

"You don't have to worry about that," she said. "I simply teach the children to stay away from the tops of the stairs."

I became red-eyed. That night, I had nightmares about Aly breaking her neck, even though she couldn't have been in better hands. Mary was wonderful, and so was her family. They were such a huge part of helping us with Aly when she was younger. We are forever grateful to them.

Faith was born on January 5, 2010. Unlike Aly, who was in a dramatic hurry to exit her mother, Faith took forever. Finally, the doctors decided to induce. This didn't work. She was eventually delivered via a Caesarean section, as was her brother, Breton, who came into this world on November 5, 2012.

As a new parent, my life was suddenly one of constant, relentless, excruciating worry. My top five irrational fears were as follows:

1. Car crashes. My wife is a good driver. But she learned how to drive in Glace Bay and has never enjoyed driving in the big city. She also hates driving at night. And so, I became frantic whenever she went on a car trip with our three kids. I'd text her continually, which is ironic, since answering the texts would have resulted in the unsafe driving that I so feared.

2. Choking. The thing you have to understand is that, when you are anxious, your thought patterns become highly specific. Though I worried about all the things that kids commonly choke on—grapes, coins, chunks of potato, marbles—I didn't worry about them that much. Instead, I

focused my hysteria on hard candy. If a box of Jolly Rancher candy made its way into the house, I would be quick to dispose of them. One of the kids would ask, "Where are those Jolly Ranchers I just got?" "No idea," I'd reply. "They are choking hazards, anyway. You don't need them."

3. Staph infections. A child has a cut, swims in salt water and ends up losing a leg. It happens rarely, but in the mind of a hypochondriac, "rarely" translates to "all the time." And so, whenever one of my kids had a cut, I'd remind them: "Don't ever go into the ocean with an open cut. You could lose your leg." While it's true, it's also highly unlikely and accomplishes little beyond turning them into worrywarts like me. But I can't help it. The words just sort of come out, all on their own.

4. The developmental effects of letting your child sleep in your bed at a wholly inappropriate age. This one, by the way, is child-specific. All three started sleeping with us. It's easier for the mother—baby cries, Mum rolls over, feeding ensues, we all know this. Aly quit the bed early. Faith did the same. Breton is ten and still sometimes crawls in with us. No one, it seems, can tell us whether this is bad or not. He says he's scared. I say he's full of it. He wins.

5. Poor diet. My children hate fruits and vegetables. Breton, in fact, will only eat four foods: french

fries, chicken fingers, peanut butter on toast and pizza. Again, this is not their fault. It's mine. I'm the same way. I rarely eat vegetables; thank God for "drinkable powdered vegetables." Every morning when I was in high school, I'd tell my mother I didn't want breakfast. Then, on the way to school, I'd stop at a local muffin shop called Treats. There, I'd buy six large chocolate chip cookies and eat them on the way to school. I did this every day for five years, Grades 9 through 13. It's hard to believe I'm alive to even type this. And as I mentioned earlier, lunch wasn't any better. It bears repeating: when it comes to children, everything you were, they are.

I admit it. I feel like I have made them worriers. Fortunately, they make friends easily. They all enjoy sports. They're well mannered and fun. They're all good at public speaking. All three are avid volleyball players. I think they like it because it's a very positive game; I can't think of another sport in which your teammates give you a high-five even when you screw up. They, in turn, are positive people. For all my worries, I'm a positive person as well. Could they have gotten that from me? They're also happy people. Again, I ask, could that be my influence? When they were children, I'd always ask them to tell me three things they were excited about. It could be something small, like ice cream for dessert, or a big thing, like a trip to Florida. I just wanted them to be appreciative of life. I like to think that it worked. *I'm* appreciative—I don't know why, I just am—and it could be that this quality would've rubbed off on them, even if we never played the things-you're-excited-about game.

The bottom line is that I've always tried to stay on top of the things that make my kids happy. We do this thing called the one-to-ten game, in which I name something and they give me a rating. Volleyball always scores high, in the neighbourhood of nine or ten. The other day, I asked Breton what he thought of hockey. He gave it a negative one thousand. This is just something I've learned to accept.

So, have I been a good parent? To answer this fairly, I do have to weigh my good parenting traits against the ways in which I've utterly failed.

1. iPads. We used them as babysitters. Even though we've never read parenting books, we do know that this is a terrible idea—today, we're having a particularly hard time prying Breton away from his. So why did we do it? Remember: these were the days when we had no help, and no time. I was always on the road, and Heather was left alone with three young ones. If she handed over a device, it's because she was trying to survive. Fortunately, I got them all blue-light glasses because I read something about how the light from screens could affect their eyes. And their brains. And their lifespans.

2. We bought them a lot of stuff. If they wanted something, they pretty much got it. They may disagree with this, but that's only because they remember the rare occasion when we didn't indulge them—I never bought them a pony, and I put my foot down on anything that they would grow out of soon. But they got everything else. You only have to look inside our garage for evidence. When Aly was into golf, I bought her a brand new set of clubs at age eight. I also bought her a brand new set at age ten. I bought her another set at age twelve. Golf clubs come in different lengths, and the thing about children is that they just don't stop growing. Now I have a garage full of golf clubs of various sizes. My grandchildren don't know it yet, but they will be golfers.

3. My kids have it too easy. I had a paper route at age ten. That was my chore. It was a job. My children do no chores and no jobs. In fact, they're starting to assign *us* chores. The other day, my son texted Heather from his bedroom, saying that he wanted some peanut butter on toast. She made the toast and brought it to him. Actually, there *is* one thing, and one thing only, that we asked them to do: I've had three cubbies built in the mud room. When each of them comes home from practice, they are supposed to put away their water bottle, their volleyball shoes and their knee pads. Mind you, there are no consequences

if they don't, other than us badgering them. Though it took a while, they eventually started to do it. That lasted about two months. The cubbies are now used to store anything that doesn't fit into any of the other storage areas in the house.

4. I forced things I liked down their throats. I did this any way I could. I wanted them to play golf for the simple reason that I loved to play golf. So I bought a golf simulator, an indoor putting green and, believe it or not, a house on a golf course in Florida. (This worked with Aly. Or, at least, it worked until the day came when she decided she'd had enough and quit.) Another example: I wanted them to play hockey for the sole reason that *I* loved to play hockey. I purchased a synthetic indoor rink. I bought passing aids and stick-handling aids and training videos. When this didn't work, I waged psychological warfare. "Hey, Breton," I'd say, "doesn't your friend Ryan like hockey? Why don't you ask him what league he plays in, and we'll sign you up for that one as well?" This didn't work. I should never have done it. It was bad parenting. And yet, you do have to encourage them from time to time—they only played volleyball because I suggested it, and now they like it. So it's tricky. If nothing else, parenting is a game of finesse.

5. We were critical of their friends. If we felt that one of their friends was rude, we told them. If we

didn't like one of their friends, we let them know. If we thought a schoolmate was bad news, we actually used that term. Oddly enough, this is probably the only parenting technique that I borrowed from my parents. It didn't work then, either.

So, there they are: the things I think I've done right, and the things I know I've done wrong. Do I have regrets over my failings? Of course I do. Every parent does. Yet I try not to be too hard on myself. There is one thing that really bothers me, however. I wish I could tell you that I remember the first time I laid eyes on my children, and the first time I held my children, and the first time that my children smiled at me. I can't. Those images aren't in my brain, even though I know they all happened. I should have forced myself to stop and form a memory. But I didn't. Basically, my career has been a trade-off. I worked all the time when they were little. Now, I work when I want to, and I spend *a lot* of time with them. The other day, I drove them to Michigan to watch a college volleyball game. It takes a lot of time to drive from Toronto to Michigan, and if I can do that now, it's because I made so many sacrifices when they were little. I tell myself this whenever I have regrets about being away so much when they were younger. It helps, but just not enough.

Oddly, there is one distinct memory I have from when Aly was a toddler. I was in the den, watching television. She kept poking her head into the room and saying, "Hello, Daddy." She thought this was great fun. I had just come home from a tour somewhere and badly needed rest. Still, it made me laugh. She just kept saying it again and again: "Hello, Daddy! Hello, Daddy! Hello, Daddy!" and each time I'd chuckle. Suddenly, I had a vision—no doubt brought on by exhaustion and an overactive imagination. I pictured her as a sixteen-year-old, asking for the car keys. I saw everything: how she'd look, how she'd act, how she'd talk. That was fourteen years ago. She's fifteen now, and everything I saw, she is.

Every day, I tell my kids I love them. This wasn't something my parents did, or parents of that generation did. So I say it a lot. When they play sports, they will often look to me in the stands from the fairway or the field. We have this little thing we do. I point to my eyes, and then my heart, and then I point to them. Eyes, heart, point. "I. Love. You." They will respond with the same, and hold up two fingers at the end. It's just something I started when Aly was golfing alone in tournaments and I couldn't be next to her. I knew the stress she was going through, and it was my way of saying, "I'm right here." I will always be right here.

# ACKNOWLEDGEMENTS

That's it. You now know everything about me, and more. I never liked writing essays in school, but this, this was much easier. I'm lying—this was hard. I don't know how to type at all, so it took forever. And the word count! This is a lot of words. My vocabulary is not that big, so I'm amazed I got this far. Heck, I'm amazed *you* got this far. You're still reading this? Thank you.

I hope you got to know me a bit more, and I hope you learned a little bit about a career in entertainment. It's not always glamorous, but it's certainly . . . well . . . entertaining.

I have so much to be thankful for, and my family and friends are at the top of that list. It takes a village, as they say, and my village was supportive, funny and helpful.

To my parents, John and Alice: I'd be nowhere without the sacrifices you made for all of us. You put our lives first in everything you did. You might not have had much, but you had humour and you passed it on to me.

To my sister, Angela: Thanks for always throwing ideas by me and listening to mine. You're just as funny, so it always helped. But most of all, thanks for always being there for your "little brother." I realize more now how fortunate I was when you were a teenager and I was younger and you would still hang out with me. Or when you would sit and colour with me or sing with me when I was little. I remember it all so well, and I'm so lucky to have you.

To my brother, Kevin: Thanks for making me laugh so much over the years. This could easily be a book about your comedy career had you chosen that path. Thanks for always looking out for me my whole life. From the playground in grade school through to university, you always protected me in every way.

To my kids: You bring me so much joy every day. You make me laugh, and I'm so glad to share this journey with you. I hope you are always able to use laughter to get you through your own lives. It's the greatest gift in the world. Nothing excites me more in life now than watching you succeed. I hope you all fall in love with something the way I did and pursue it to the highest level.

Big thanks to Robert Hough, Jim Gifford and everyone at HarperCollins for their help and guidance to get this to print. Tracking down a comic who has attention deficit disorder and probably some obsessive-compulsive disorder is no easy task. Or maybe I have neither of those, but I'm sure I have something. At least it's not Lyme disease—yet.

# ACKNOWLEDGEMENTS

Thanks to Steve Mason, Jerry MacPhee, James and John Macciocchi, Dave O'Connor, Tim Korba and Randy Urban. These guys all came to shows when I was starting out—those were the hardest times as a comic, the early years. They are all funny, and that helped, too. And they always reminded me when *I* was funny. That was a big help. With ideas and concepts and yes, even jokes. Being able to bounce ideas and bits off friends was so helpful because they were always so honest and funny. Thanks, guys.

Finally, thanks to my wife, Heather. You are my first test on any material, and sometimes it involves you! It can't be easy being married to a comedian, and your love and support are unmatched. You complete me.

I don't know where my career will take me next, and that's exciting. But I do know that whatever happens, most of all I'm gonna laugh. Laugh, laugh, laugh.